David Curry

Tom Murphy
Plays: Three

**The Morning After Optimism, The Sanctuary Lamp,
The Gigli Concert**

The Morning After Optimism introduces fairytale characters with
consciously artifical language and explores the relationship
between illusion and freedom.

The Sanctuary Lamp 'A lyrical play about spiritual refugees . . .
Mr Murphy writes speeches that are really arias – long rhythmic
excursions that turn the language of the slums into a kind of
poetry.' *New York Times*

The Gigli Concert 'A complex and fascinating play bearing the
true stigmata of talent.' Michael Billington, *Guardian*

'Sends you reeling and exhilarated from the theatre.' *Financial
Times*

Tom Murphy's work includes the internationally acclaimed *A
Whistle in the Dark* (Theatre Royal, Stratford East, 1961, Long
Wharf Theatre, New Haven, Connecticut and New York, Royal
Court, London, 1989), *Famine* (Peacock Theatre, Dublin, 1968,
Royal Court, London, 1969), *Bailegangaire* (Druid Theatre
Company, Galway, 1985, Donmar Warehouse, London, 1986,
BBC Radio, 1987) winner of the Harvey's Best Play Award and
the Sunday Tribune Theatre Award 1985–6, *Too Late for Logic*
(Abbey Theatre, Dublin, 1989) and *The Patriot Game* (Peacock
Theatre, Dublin, 1991). He was born in Tuam, County Galway.
During the sixties he lived in London and now lives in Dublin.
He is a member of Aosdána and the Irish Academy of Letters.

D1571076

by the same author

On the Outside
On the Inside
A Whistle in the Dark
A Crucial Week in the Life of a Grocer's Assistant
The Orphans
Famine
The Morning after Optimism
The White House
The Vicar of Wakefield (adaptation)
The J. Arthur Maginnis Story
The Sanctuary Lamp
The Blue Macushla
The Informer (adaptation)
Conversations on a Homecoming
Bailegangaire
A Thief of a Christmas
Too Late for Logic
The Patriot Game
The Gigli Concert
The Seduction of Morality (a novel)

David Curry

TOM MURPHY

Plays: Three

The Morning After Optimism
The Sanctuary Lamp
The Gigli Concert

with an introduction by Fintan O'Toole

Methuen Drama

METHUEN WORLD CLASSICS

This collection first published in Great Britain 1994
by Methuen Drama
an imprint of Reed Consumer Books Ltd
Michelin House, 81 Fulham Road, London SW3 6RB
and Auckland, Melbourne, Singapore and Toronto
and distributed in the United States of America by HEB Inc.,
361 Hanover Street, Portsmouth, New Hampshire NH 03801 3959

The Morning After Optimism first published by the Mercier Press
1973 and revised for this edition. Copyright © 1973, 1994 by
Tom Murphy
The Sanctuary Lamp first published by The Gallery Press 1976 and
revised for this edition. Copyright © 1976, 1984, 1994 by Tom
Murphy
The Gigli Concert first published by Methuen Drama 1988 in *After
Tragedy*, revised and reissued in the Methuen Modern Plays edition in
1991 and further revised for this edition. Copyright © 1988, 1991,
1994 by Tom Murphy

This collection copyright © 1994 by Tom Murphy
Introduction copyright © 1994 by Methuen Drama

The author has asserted his moral rights.

ISBN 0–413–68350–8

A CIP catalogue record for this book is available from the British
Library

Photoset by Wilmaset Ltd, Wirral
Printed and bound in Great Britain
by Cox & Wyman Ltd, Reading, Berkshire

Caution
These plays are fully protected by copyright. Any enquiries
concerning rights for professional or amateur stage productions
should be addressed to Alexandra Cann Representation,
337 Fulham Road, London SW10 9TW.
No performance may be given unless a licence has been obtained.

This paperback is sold subject to the condition that it shall not, by
way of trade or otherwise, be lent, resold, hired out or otherwise
circulated without the publisher's prior consent in any form of
binding or cover other than that in which it is published and
without a similar condition including this condition being imposed
on the subsequent purchaser.

Contents

Tom Murphy:
A Chronology

A Whistle in the Dark, Theatre Royal, Stratford East	1961
On the Outside (with Noel O'Donoghue), Radio Eireann	1962
Famine, Peacock Theatre	1968
The Orphans, Gate Theatre	1968
A Crucial Week in the Life of a Grocer's Assistant, Abbey Theatre	1969
The Morning After Optimism, Abbey Theatre	1971
The White House, Abbey Theatre	1972
On the Inside, Project Arts Centre	1974
The Vicar of Wakefield (adaptation), Abbey Theatre	1974
The Sanctuary Lamp, Abbey Theatre	1976
The J. Arthur Maginnis Story, Irish Theatre Company	1976
Epitaph under Ether (compilation from Synge), Abbey Theatre	1979
The Blue Macushla, Abbey Theatre	1980
The Informer (adaptation), Olympia Theatre	1981
She Stoops to Conquer (Irish setting), Abbey Theatre	1982
The Gigli Concert, Abbey Theatre	1983
Conversations on a Homecoming, Druid Theatre	1985
Bailegangaire, Druid Theatre	1985
A Thief of a Christmas, Abbey Theatre	1985
Too Late for Logic, Abbey Theatre	1989
The Patriot Game, Peacock Theatre	1991
The Seduction of Morality (a novel, pub. Abacus)	1994

Introduction

In thinking about these plays, the image that comes to mind is one that seems unconnected. It is not a theatrical image at all, but a painting, albeit a particularly dramatic one. It is Tintoretto's great painting 'The Annunciation', of the moment at which the Angel erupts into the life of the Virgin Mary. Most paintings of the scene are bathed in awe and submission, doing homage to the condescension of the Eternal which has deigned to grace our dull world with its fleeting presence. Tintoretto's, on the other hand, is so forceful as to be brutal. The Angel is crashing in through the wall, followed by a battering ram of cherubs. The world we glimpse behind him is an apocalyptic wreck, dark with chaos. Inside, in a mundane house with neat wicker chairs and scrubbed tile floors, Mary is falling backwards, terrified, transfixed. Her home, her sanctuary, has been invaded. The Eternal has burst into her life without warning or invitation, not a visitor but an outrage, and she will never be the same again. The painting comes to mind because if Tom Murphy were a painter you know that he would imagine the Annunciation like this. Since he is a playwright, his vision of flight and home, of ordinary humanity assaulted by eternal forces is, instead, in these plays.

These are plays of flight and sanctuary. We catch their characters on the run, somewhere between fear and hope, between a need to run away and a desire to find a safe place to hide. And we also catch their language, their sense of theatrical form, on the hop. Like their characters, the plays themselves are out on the edge, cut loose from the known world and let loose into wild territory. They hover above ground, close enough to be part of the familiar landscape, yet never quite coming to rest in the mundane. Written over more than 20 years, they yet have a remarkable coherence in the broad shape they take, the search for and final achievement of something beyond either restless flight or illusory home.

All three plays are dominated by middle-aged men who have been impelled to go on journeys away from home and out of their depth. James in *The Morning After Optimism* is literally on the run, a comically exaggerated villain in flight from his crimes, seeking refuge in a fairytale forest. Harry in *The Sanctuary Lamp* is holed up in a church like a mediaeval outlaw, hoping to keep at bay the pain and guilt of his messy life. JPW King in *The Gigli Concert* is a kind of cross between Dr Livingstone and Robinson Crusoe, a missionary who has become a shipwrecked loner, an Englishman sent to Dublin by a cult to convert the natives, and left there, beached and bereft.

In one sense, then, these are plays of exile. At a simplistic biographical level, it can be noted of the three plays that Murphy wrote them at three stages of his career and that somewhere behind them lies his journey from Ireland to England and back again. *The Morning After Optimism*, which he started writing in 1962 (though it was not staged until 1971), is the first of his plays to be written in England, where he emigrated after the success of *A Whistle in the Dark* in 1961, and its sense of going out beyond the world of childhood to slay dragons and witches reflects that. *The Sanctuary Lamp* is his first full-length play to be entirely written after his return to Ireland in 1970, and its search for a santuary is probably coloured by that return. And *The Gigli Concert* continues in some ways to reflect on the duality of exile, having enormous fun with the sterotypes of Irishman and Englishman.

These facts are not irrelevant but they could be misleading. It is important that Ireland and England feature largely in the plays (even the contrast between the 'real' and fairytale characters in *The Morning After Optimism* contains a playful suggestion of linguistic contrast between Irish and English speech). It is also important that the quest in both *Gigli* and *The Sanctuary Lamp* is engaged in by English, not Irish, characters. There is a feeling in these plays that the originality of form and language that marks them off from so much of contemporary Irish writing for the theatre owes something to the refusal of local colour and familiarity implicit in an Irish writer creating, not merely English characters, but English protagonists. More profoundly, the deliberate crossing of boundaries in the plays, the refusal of opposites to hold their distinctions, takes the form of a subversion of notions of what is typically Irish or English.

But these are not naturalistic plays, and the relationship they bear to exile and to the overwrought interpenetrations of neighbouring islands is much more complex than might be implied in a pointing up of such background features. For one thing, the question of Irishness and Englishness pales somewhat when you remember that these are, above all, European plays, profoundly engaged with the archetypes of western culture. For another, while the notion of exile at work in the plays is undoubtedly rooted in the shapes the writer's life has taken, its visible blossomings in the plays are more metaphysical than sociological, more mythic than geographic.

To grasp the first of these points, it is necessary merely to mention some of the more obvious connections to the European hinterland. *The Morning After Optimism* draws on Shakespeare's Forest of Arden for its setting, on Jungian psychology for its imagery, and on European fairytale for much of its shape, language and action. *The Sanctuary Lamp* is to a large extent a version of *The Oresteia* with Biblical overtones, with Harry at times an Orestes, at others an Agamemnon, and again at others a Samson among the Philistines. *The Gigli Concert* makes obvious use of the voice and aura of the Italian tenor Beniamino Gigli. Less obviously, the template it works from is Goethe's *Faust* and through it the play refers back to a European tradition of alchemy, magic and defiance. The Irish/English dynamic in the plays should not be allowed to distract from their essential nature as European theatre, consciously playing on and with a set of European cultural archetypes.

And at the same time, the reflection on exile in the plays also has as much to do with these archetypes as it has with a writer's journey from Tuam to London to Dublin. There are Murphy plays – *A Whistle in the Dark, A Crucial Week in the Life of a Grocer's Assistant, Conversations on a Homecoming* – which are directly about exile and return. Those plays are immediately social in their context. But the plays in this volume represent another layer of Murphy's work, one in which the immediate social world has receded into the background and the question of exile has become itself archetypal, itself a kind of shaping myth. It is still worth knowing that emigration and exile are central, even defining, aspects of modern Irish experience, but that knowledge is less immediately applicable to what happens in these plays.

The shift can be measured in the most directly theatrical way imaginable – through the notion of space. Whereas in the other Murphy plays, the space of the stage is relatively naturalistic – a suburban house, a small town street, a pub – here the space is much more consciously theatrical. In each of these plays, space is theatrically enriched. Though two of them have what might look like conventional settings, it does not take long to realise that we are in the theatrical space, not of Ibsen or Chekhov, but of Meyerhold or Yeats, where the stage is also a kind of altar or church, a ritualised area where everything becomes possible, where the laws of cause and effect break down and, if the spells are right or the prayers are sufficiently heartfelt, miracles may happen.

The difference, of course, is that Murphy habitually seeks salvation not in the elevated but in the downcast. Like Francisco in *The Sanctuary Lamp* his Saviour is one who calls the goats to his side and banishes the sheep into eternal damnation. The churches of such a faith are downbeat, comic places, and Murphy gives us as much a mockery of as a search for the sacred. The Forest of Arden is also a tourist trap where Rosie suggests that she and James should occupy one of the many cabins for rent. It is a deliberately mundane fairyland. The church in *The Sanctuary Lamp* may be consecrated ground but it is occupied by a disillusioned priest, a Jewish strongman on the run, a foul-mouthed Irish blasphemer and a deluded young girl. JPW King's 'dynamatologist's' office may be a kind of church but it is a church without worshippers, without faith and without a priest. The plays may be intense, but they are also intensely funny, and much of the humour is in the naked disjunction between the people and their place, between heroic aspiration and absurd reality. We are in a world where a ponce may kill a fairytale prince, where the nearest equivalents to Greek heroes are circus performers, where a great alchemist is really a middle-aged loser out of his mind on drink and drugs, trying to sing like an Italian tenor.

Yet what makes Murphy a great playwright is that he is not content to undercut the myths and is driven to re-invent them. In this, Murphy is one of the few heirs to Joyce in Irish writing, not because there are any similarities of language or form, but because, like Joyce, he is interested in both bringing the myths down to size and in forcing reality up to the scale of myth. Just as Joyce domesticates Homer in Dublin, without losing the sense of scale, the epic ambition, so Murphy does with Faust and Orestes. His reductions are not merely reductive but also the making of a dangerous and subversive connection between the world of archetype and myth and the world we live in, a connection in which our world is weighed in the balance and found wanting. That James in *Optimism* is not his fantasy-self Edmund; that Harry is not a Greek hero but a lost soul; that JPW is not a magician – these are criticisms of the world as it is as much as they are comic undercuttings of human illusion. If, in Murphy, to hold on to illusion is to be doomed, then equally to be incapable of illusion is to be incapable of redemption. To put it another way, disillusion in these plays, is a prelude, not to resignation but to salvation.

The world of these plays, then is mythic, but not heroic. They bring us into dreams, fantasies, impossibilities. But the dreams are like the day-dreams that the philosopher Ernst Bloch distinguishes from night-dreams: 'The dream is thought of mostly as night dream. However, we dream not only at night; the day is also interwoven with dreams. . . . Between the two there exist considerable differences: principally in the fact that the ego does not disappear in the day dream. On the contrary it is there very actively, and does not exercise any sort of censorship, with the result that wishes function even better in the day dream, more visibly than in the night dream, not disguised, but shameless, uninhibitedly open, often daring, and with a grudge.' These plays are those sorts of day dreams, wide-awake dreams where yearnings and desires, obsessions and fantasies make their way onto the stage, not slyly and lyrically, but with a harsh ungainly insistence, with a grudge. In spite of being life's losers, indeed precisely because that is what they are, the people in the plays are gripped by yearnings more concrete and immediate than any fixed reality could be.

The full measure of Murphy's insistence on the interpenetration of the life we yearn for with the life we live is that the play which looks most ambitious here is actually in some ways the least ambitious. *The Morning After Optimism* is certainly no ordinary play, with its consciously artificial language, its use of fairytale characters, and its exploration of the relationship between illusion and freedom. What is striking, though, is that Murphy became more adventurous, not by making his plays more avant-garde, but by making them, ostensibly at least, less so. *Optimism* proclaims itself, by its setting, by its use of characters who dress and talk like they are well acquainted with the Brothers Grimm, for what it is: a play of the dream world. By contrast, the other two plays in this volume look like a step backwards into some kind of realism. In fact, however, both are much more radical. By giving us the appearance of a recognisable world, by seeming to accept 'reality' they do something much more daring than *Optimism* does. They present a reality that is already imbued with dreams, saturated in possibilities and impossibilities. Like the Angel coming through the wall, they take us unawares.

With *The Sanctuary Lamp*, we get a modern play that has the scale of ambition of the Greeks. It is not just that the play is a version of sorts of *The Oresteia* with Harry starting out as the Orestes of *Eumenides*, seeking sanctuary in the temple of Apollo from the Furies that pursue him, becoming Agamemnon haunted by the death of his daughter, and becoming again Orestes bent on revenge. More importantly, it is that Murphy follows the Greek original in seeking to make a play about nothing less than the replacement of the old gods by the new, of worn-out Christianity by a new faith in man.

With *The Gigli Concert*, arguably Murphy's masterpiece, we get something even more ambitious, a full-scale dramatisation of the impossible. With one set and three characters, Murphy gives us an operatic drama complete with deaths and arias, a version of *Faust* in which the Irishman's Mephistopheles temps JPW into taking on his own demonic striving, and in which against all the laws of reality this down-at-heel alchemist finds the philosopher's stone of despair that enables him to transmute the leaden metal of his life into a moment of pure, glittering possibility. When he sings, it also a hymn to the theatre itself, to that darkness in which, 'alive in time at the same time' we encounter the possibility that everything might happen if only we are in the presence of an imagination courageous and expansive enough to defy the odds. With Murphy we are, and when JPW opens his windows at the end of the play and lets in the morning light, we know that we have been with one of the few playwrights now writing who is able to let the full, unfiltered light of European culture in on his plays and not be dazzled by the glare.

Fintan O'Toole
Dublin, 1994

The Morning After Optimism

Characters

JAMES, a ponce (pimp), temporarily retired: his mother died
recently
ROSIE, a whore, his girl friend
EDMUND, a young poet with an archaic gimmick
ANASTASIA, an orphan

A forest.
Introductory and bridging music from Symphonie Fantastique
(Berlioz)

The Morning After Optimism was first performed at The Abbey Theatre, 15 March 1971 with the following cast:

ROSIE	Eithne Dunne
JAMES	Colin Blakely
ANASTASIA	Nuala Hayes
EDMUND	Bryan Murray

Directed by Hugh Hunt
Designed by Bronwen Casson
Lighting by Leslie Scott

to the memory of
Tom Naughton

Scene One

Symponie Fantastique (Berlioz) introduces the play and bridges the scenes.
A forest. The tree-trunks reach up so high that we do not see the branches.

The cawing of a crow, then ROSIE and JAMES enter. ROSIE is carrying a suitcase. She stops, waits for instructions. JAMES, unencumbered, is looking back to see if they are being followed.

JAMES is middle-aged and neurotic. His spivish dress is exaggerated: short-backed jacket, dickie-bow, crepe-soled shoes; a moustache. His 'evil' is self-lacerating. Suddenly he races across the stage to check the opposite direction for a pursuer: after a few moments he races back across the stage again and off. (His running and posing are stylised: running at breakneck speed, or trotting daintily, feigning cockiness; posing, taking stances as if to say his body is a dangerous weapon; at other times his stance wilting pathetically.)

Seeing that instructions are not forthcoming, ROSIE takes the initiative. She opens the suitcase and produces two stools. The suitcase is convertible and is turned into a table equipped with aluminium legs. The table and stools are a matching suite.

ROSIE is 37. Her dress suggests a dated whore. Her catering for JAMES is a mixture of sympathy, insecurity and malice. She takes refuge in self-deceit.

JAMES enters racing across the stage through the trees, and off, checking again for pursuers.

ROSIE produces two plastic cups and a bottle of gin from her large handbag. She pours a little gin into each mug. She looks about, unsure as to where JAMES *is. She calls:*

ROSIE. It's ready!

> JAMES *enters, his run slowing to a cocky trot. He sits tensely, ignoring his gin. The forest towering around them.* ROSIE *sighs, feigning contentment.* JAMES *winces at her effort. After a moment she tries again, hopefully conversational:*

This is a funny looking forest, James.

JAMES (*whispering, indulging in alarm*). What forest? Where? . . . What's funny about it?

ROSIE. I don't know.

JAMES. Then what are you talking about? (*Pause.*) Do you not like the look of it?

ROSIE. Like, I'm not sure. What do you think of it?

JAMES. I don't think anything of it! Now! I will not be made a fool of!

> *Pause.*

ROSIE. Oh, there's a little village over there —

JAMES. Seen it, poxy village!

ROSIE. Still, it's quiet.

JAMES. Girls there dressed up in puppy-fat, I suppose.

ROSIE. You put an over-emphasis on girls, James.

JAMES. Not thro' choice.

ROSIE. No, not through choice.

JAMES. But — not — anymore. Now!

ROSIE. Still, it's out of the way, what do you say? Off the beaten track so to speak.

JAMES. It would suit me to see them all as ugly as porridge.

ROSIE. And perhaps we could rent a little cabin for the interim.

JAMES. Hairy faces and turkeys' craws. What?

ROSIE. As ugly as sin, James.

JAMES. Mouths like torn pockets. Now!

Suddenly, JAMES *is trotting about again to see if they are being followed:*

Bastard, 'Feathers'!

ROSIE. No, we're safe, James.

JAMES. But I've got a trick or two up my sleeve.

ROSIE. That last bit of cross-country was a brilliant notion.

JAMES. . . . Whoever he is.

ROSIE. Whatever he wants, James.

JAMES. I know he hasn't got money for me anyway. (*A grim laugh.*) A pot of gold.

ROSIE. Oh, that's very funny, James. (*Going into an old routine, a sort of song and shuffle, to amuse him.*) My name is Rose-ee, Rose-ee! James! I'm widely known and popular! —

JAMES (*hurtful*). Once upon a time — once upon a time.

ROSIE. . . . Okay, once upon a time.

JAMES (*to himself*). Once upon a time.

ROSIE. Popularity waning! —

JAMES. Wear and tear.

ROSIE. I admit it.

JAMES. Yeh?

ROSIE. . . . I'm not too per-tic-ular-like, no more! I'm not too
per-pen-dicular! No conditions! –

JAMES. One condition (*Money*.)

ROSIE. Only one condition. (*New material, inspired, to
herself.*) My brains are danced on like grapes to make
abortions!

He laughs. She is pleased.

I say my head is sore! (*They laugh.*)
My belly is a tub of moss! (*They laugh.*)
Yo-ho-ho and the tits are for whom!

The laughter subsiding.

JAMES. I've been everybody's victim for too long.

ROSIE. Far too long. Tell us a really filthy story, James.

JAMES. Magic-mirror-on-the-wall, who is the fairest of them
all!

They laugh again.

I'll tell you a story.

ROSIE. Yes. (*She has heard it before.*)

JAMES. I'm standing on my usual corner.

ROSIE. A Monday night.

JAMES. A Monday night, business is bad, I'm about to go
home and enjoin you myself.

ROSIE. A wind comes up.

JAMES. A newspaper billowing, coming round the corners,
deserting a lamp-post to wrap itself around my ankles. Now,
what is the thought in my mind as I bend to unravel those
sheets?

ROSIE. Blue knickers.

JAMES. Adolescent blue knickers. And the thought persists as I read 'Come home, Mother dead, foreign papers please copy'. Do you see my point?

ROSIE. The item trimmed in black meant nothing.

JAMES. Nothing. And I said to myself, you've come a long way, Jimmy kid. And I said to myself, I like it.

ROSIE. But what do you say to a little cabin for the interim?

JAMES. I couldn't care less about my mammy. Now! (*Intensely.*) And to her dead hand, so mottled brown, so worn with care, steals nightly in my bed, (*He brushes his hand across his face.*) I say, nickerdehpazzee! What?

ROSIE (*mechanically*). Nickerdehpazzee, James.

JAMES (*to himself*). Now.

ROSIE. But what do you say to a little cabin?

JAMES (*to himself*). Yeh know.

ROSIE (*to herself*). What is your suggestion, I feel so guilty, once upon a time I knew the name of every single bird.

JAMES. But could you recognise them?

ROSIE. I could.

JAMES. Well, it would suit me if someone came along and stabbed the lot of them.

ROSIE. Once I knew every flower.

JAMES. And everyone knows they are covered in fleas.

In the background, ANASTASIA entering: glimpses of her walking through the trees, a water urn in her hand. She is a beautiful barefooted girl of about seventeen, her dress ragged in the most becoming way. She does not see them: they do not see her. She exits.

ROSIE. Yes. I think you should just sit right down and have a good cry. For yourself. You feel the better for it, they say. Grief is bad at the best of times. Give vent to it. Cry to lose it.

It's an old and tested panacea. A sensible function of the tear in the purge, they say. And it is a great burier of things past. And there's nothing to be ashamed of in the male tear. And it might be cheaper on your nerves, and on mine, in the long run. And take consolation: you have tolerable earning potential (*Herself.*) and you're not finished yet. Not by a long chalk. Why properly pruned of the dead wood you could be almost anything. You could almost be yourself. And then say, non, je ne regrette rien, no I will have no regrets. And, che sera, sera, if you like. And then get on with the business of living. In any case that's what I did. And I feel the better for it.

JAMES (*grimly*). Can't say two kind words to me.

ROSIE (*absently, softly*). Otherwise it will crucify you.

JAMES. Can you?

ROSIE. Yes. I know of a person who, when she found out that things are really what they seem and not what they are supposed to be, instead of manifesting her reaction in a little tear, held back and clung to her pain. Until, one day, as she was silently hanging out the washing on the line, a gander came hissing from the end of the garden, chasing her indoors. Then she cried. She nearly died. But too late. To this day that woman believes she is a goose.

JAMES. Can't say two kind words.

ROSIE. That is, if she's still alive.

JAMES. Two kind words.

ROSIE. What?

JAMES. You thought I wasn't listening, didn't you?

ROSIE. No, I learned a lot from that woman's case history.

JAMES. You want to see me crying, don't you? Succumb. Well, you won't! You or anybody else. I've had enough! You don't know what's on my mind now, do you?

ROSIE (*fears he is thinking of leaving her*). We've been together a long time, James.

JAMES. What's that got to do with it? . . . I'm waiting here for 'Feathers'!

He trots about.

ROSIE. No, we're safe!

JAMES. No, we're not. (*Triumphantly.*) I left a trail for him to follow! (*Nervously.*) What?

ROSIE (*considers*). . . . Yes. Wait for him, see who he is, what he wants, have it out.

JAMES. What?

ROSIE. Let's have done with him.

JAMES. I've got a trick or two.

ROSIE. Since you're not afraid of him, you said.

JAMES. He's following you too.

ROSIE. Oh no, he's not, James.

JAMES (*feebly*). I've got a . . . up my sleeve . . . (*His frustration and anger overcome his fear.*) Everybody's victim! Well, not anymore! Those puppy-fat princesses! No more! And that feathered bastard shadowing me – a Monster! I'll stop him in his tracks. And that night rambling corpse of a mammy! I'll lay that dead witch sleeping! (*To* ROSIE.) Go! Rent that cabin! (*He trots about; then strikes a fighting pose.*) Yes, you're coming of age at last, Jimmy kid. Well, come on, come on, come on, dragon-feathers, try me! Just don with pride that honest evil mantle, tried and true, for this great task, Jimmy kid, and you can't lose. Keep your evil wits, don't go balloon, and do not deviate.

ROSIE *has packed the suitcase. He shouts at her.*

Go!

ROSIE *exits.*

JAMES' *stance wilting.*

Now . . . Yeh know . . . Once I saw a girl, her back in headscarf and raincoat, once. I just passed by, I didn't see her face, in my blue motorcar, and turned left for Eros and the statue of Liberty, and became ponce in the graveyard. She may have been Miss Right, she certainly was Miss Possible, cause my hidden, real, beautiful self manifested itself in a twinge . . . Just to hold her hand, yeh know.

ANASTASIA *enters background, playfully carrying the water urn on her head.*

JAMES, *unobserved by her, gaping at her. Then angry because 'Feathers' has not showed up, leaving him available for this temptation.*

Feathers! Feathers!

ANASTASIA *exits.*

JAMES *starts to follow, at first reluctantly, then breaking into a trot, then racing, taking a wide circle to intercept her. He exits.*

The lights are fading.

EDMUND *is entering, not clearly defined: a tall figure wearing a feathered Robin Hood hat.*

Scene Two

Patches of light and shade in the forest. ANASTASIA *running in circles, in fear. Off, the roars of anonymous wild animals.*

Then JAMES, *off and as he enters, shouting, as if driving away the animals.*

JAMES. Yaa hah-haa hah-haa! Yaa hah-haa, hah-haa!

JAMES *trotting towards her, unsure, smiling against his face.*

I got rid of them, rid of them, dangerous, they're gone, unfamiliar, away, now . . . Saved you, rescued, I mean, rescued, rescued, so I'm glad you were not drowning or anything like that. For I am a poor swimmer, yeh know . . . But, that's that. (*About to leave.*)

ANASTASIA. What were they?

JAMES. What – what?

ANASTASIA. My heart! What species?

JAMES. Oh!

ANASTASIA. I have not heard of animals so wild in this forest before.

JAMES. No gregarious cats were they, hah-hah!

ANASTASIA. The shock!

JAMES. Yes.

ANASTASIA. I'm grateful. (*She smiles.*)

JAMES. Yes! I mean, one of them, one of them nearly, one of them nearly bit the-the (*hand*) off me . . . But the danger's past, so Jimmy could go, and dealt with. (*She puts down the urn.*) That's a very nice jug.

ANASTASIA. Thank you.

JAMES. What? And – not at all – And – Oh, you're lovely! (*A step towards her; he pulls himself up.*) I meant –

ANASTASIA. Thank you.

JAMES. What? (*Delighted.*) I mean – You are! I meant that! You're all that! And more! Not a smelly hippy. I could tell that by your manner of speaking. Much more promising and correct. They're worse than the birds. Louse-ridden hair and feathers. 'Feathers'! (JAMES *running about again.*) This head following me, an animal from way back. I left a crimson trail. But he must be one right stupid dumb-cluck. Well, just as well for him. Never mind. But as I was saying, I suspect we've got the same values. There's an overall style about you. I ask you, style? Maxi, mini, one or the other, but the two of them

together? don't make me laugh. Twelve inches of provocative
thigh, unwashed, laid bare, fleeting glimpses, under a cold
long Russian overcoat! What for? Just to be chased, laid
waste – Do you see what I mean? Nothing lofty. Even so,
where does it get the hopeful chaser? Drop dead. I don't
speak the same language, see? Or if I do and click, it's lay-me-
down-I'm-a-dead-mutton-chick! No conversation. Nor worth
the winning. Some day my prince will come? Don't make me
laugh – they make me puke! – they do nothing for me! I walk
away and I say, thank you for the comparison. The whip I'd
give them. No, not for Jimmy here. My mother told me to
look for a bit of decorum. She used to play piano – (*Miming
pianist.*) With her hands – Unblemished then –
Nickerdehpazzee – Never mind. But she would like your style
and I certainly like your spirit. Yes, I must confess I do, and
I've been twice round the world and not by boat, which
brings me to the point I wanted to make . . . Ah . . . (*He has
forgotten the point.*) Nevertheless, what's your name, yeh
know?

ANASTASIA (*girlishly playful*). You don't know?

JAMES. Should I?

ANASTASIA. No.

JAMES. What?

ANASTASIA. Guess.

JAMES. Ah –

ANASTASIA. Yes.

JAMES. What?

ANASTASIA (*spelling*). A. N. A –

JAMES. Ann!

ANASTASIA. No. S. T. A. S. I. A.

JAMES. . . . . Anastasia! (*An impetuous step towards her, pulls himself up. Then a deliberate step away, from her.*) See? (*A trot taking him further away from her.*)See? (*She does not understand.*) . . . Rushing things. We must be careful. My father vas a Russian, my mother vas a Russian, but I, I take my time! Joke. (*She starts giggling.*) Me for you, and you for me, and tea for two and hah-hah-hah! (*He considers dancing with her, changes his mind, dances with the urn.*) A fellow and a girl in a dance hall, see? and he says to her 'Some dance!' and she says to him 'Some don't.' (*He pauses for a moment, melting at her smiling innocence. Tongue-tied.*) Ana-Ana-Ana. (*Her smile disappears, a moment of fear. He starts to dance again.*) 'It's a lovely floor' he said to her 'Why don't you dance on it?' she said to him.

He puts the urn on the ground behind him. The slightest suggestion that the urn is a hostage.

Why don't you dance on it, it's a very nice jug. Now, you might think me outspoken, but I like to think I'm direct. I like to think of a clean slate, yeh know. Why? You well may ask. As a basis for a proper little proposition. So, to come to the point, I'm coming to, Ana-Ana-Ana, a new chance is all I want. Hmm?

She giggles. He wipes his brow.

No, Ana-Ana-Ana, serious.

ANASTASIA. Sorry?

JAMES. Holidays?

ANASTASIA. I live here.

JAMES. I guessed that. Don't for a moment think I didn't. But I didn't want to ask were you a native. It might be considered a coarse word. But now, nevertheless, what I mean to say, yeh know, is this, so, what do you say to that?

ANASTASIA. I'm an orphan.

JAMES. Aaa.

ANASTASIA. I've been alone for some time and long to be found.

JAMES. Aa, I am very lonely too. And there is no other?

ANASTASIA. Not as yet.

JAMES. We have an awful lot in common.

ANASTASIA (*smiles*). Yes.

JAMES. What?

ANASTASIA. Yes.

JAMES. And I'm free! Totally free!

ANASTASIA. But do not misunderstand –

JAMES. See how easy it is to talk to me?

ANASTASIA } But do not –
JAMES   } Shh, and listen! . . . Didn't you hear a solitary
             bird sing over there just now?

ANASTASIA. A what?

JAMES. An omen . . . I don't really dislike the birds. Yeh know. Yeh know. Not when I'm happy. I have nice thoughts, see. I wouldn't stab them. The crow is my friend. It's nice to run one's fingers through one's hair, hmm? It's nice to run one's fingers through your hair, hmm? Let me run my fingers through your hair only?

ANASTASIA. What nonsense!

JAMES (*staggered*). What – what? A fella and a girl in a dance hall, see, and –

ANASTASIA (*nervously*). You are being foolish.

JAMES. No I'm not. If you're worried about – about, well, I won't. Not without your consent – Not at all! But before you speak, Ana-Ana-Ana, have to play it fair, want to play it straight, cause today is now or never – Would you like to hear the story of my life? I'll erase it as I talk, for the slate,

clean slate, tabula rasa or caput. I've known the bluest score,
I've had the biggest ball, but don't jump to conclusions, no
don't make me laugh, never irretrievably lost, yeh know . . .
The permissive society? I was a member, when that club was
exclusive, when 'twas dangerous to be in it, when the tension
was there. And I might have got lost, but they threw open the
doors, didn't they? The amateurs came in to desecrate with
innocence; everybody in, doing it with flowers; the pros were
in despair, the cons were in confusion – Pollen, pollen
everywhere! – There was too much of it about to go around!
Do you see what I mean? I uttered a prayer, Jesus, Mary and
Joseph, where is the sin any more, I said! . . . Irretrievably –
irretrievably lost never . . . So, shacked up with Rosie, tried
to figure it all out, but something had depressed me, took to
looking at the ceiling, and while wrestling with morality, put
Rosie on the game. (*Reflective.*) Yeh know . . . And I could
have expanded. I could have been the very best. Why, they
napped *me* to be the berries in my trade! But that was me
always: Played it along with the single cow – Why? You well
may ask again – when I could have had twenty top-notch
harlots in my stall. I'll tell you why, I've just worked it all
out! I was practising *monogomy* for when the real thing came
along. As promised. See, I've thought of you a lot. Anastasia
was the name whispered by the wind. Hmm? (*She looks
frightened for a moment.*) Oh, but do not get me wrong, it
was not that straight and narrow, and we agreed the cleanest
slate for our little proposition: I tell all . . . If you had seen
me, on the quiet, having my slice, on any old side, with any
old whore, you'd have called me Ping-Pong: From Biddy to
Jackie, scrubber to moohair, penthouse to doorway,
pickpocketing their pennies while engaged in the act. But that
was me always, never committed: Those sorties were swift.
Well, the wind would start whispering, Hans Christian
Anderson, and I'd go back to my base, for another session
with the ceiling, always descending, the walls closing in, and
my ideals always, my ideals always, my ideals always,
suffering insomnia! And here I am. As you can very well see.
Today, I am glad I kept my ideals. Oh, have no doubts about

that. And as from now, I've forgotten everything I know. And don't you think with your pretty little head – with your pretty little head, I haven't. And now I would like, I would like, I would like, I would like to combine with your sweet self from scratch. Hmmm?

ANASTASIA. I must go now.

She starts to move to retrieve the urn. JAMES lunges instinctively to stop her. ANASTASIA is terrified. JAMES is horrified that they have reached this impasse.

JAMES. No, I can make you happy, I can make you laugh! –

ANASTASIA. No! No! –

JAMES. We had some laughs, remember? My father vas a –

ANASTASIA. No! No! –

JAMES. Look what's this, what's this? (*He is imitating a hen.*)

ANASTASIA. Though I am orphaned in this world –

JAMES. A hen, a hen!

ANASTASIA. Do not think that any farmyard plan of yours –

JAMES. What's this, what's this? (*The sounds of the anonymous wild animals that we heard at the start of the scene. He realises his mistake.*)

ANASTASIA. . . . . Can frighten or –

JAMES. That was not to frighten you! –

ANASTASIA. Distort the picture of my hope –

JAMES. An innocent way of getting to meet you!

ANASTASIA. For I have dreamed of one who'll come to these woods and find me –

JAMES. No good to me by intimidation!

ANASTASIA. A man with eyes flaming green –

JAMES. No good to me by force!

ANASTASIA. Burning equally for righteousness and love for me –

JAMES. I'm prepared to tie my feet together! –

ANASTASIA. His dark abundant tresses –

JAMES. If such should be your wont! –

ANASTASIA. Falling in natural disarray –

JAMES. Listen, listen, listen –

ANASTASIA. His shining purest youth –

JAMES. The point I wanted to make! –

ANASTASIA. Being acknowledged even by the grass that loves his thread –

JAMES. Don't keep thinking about sex!

ANASTASIA. So slender, so certain, so perfect –

JAMES. I consider it a secondary thing –

ANASTASIA. So tall.

JAMES (*his head rolling in confusion*). A secondary thing – a secondary thing! Had I considered it a primarary thing – a primarary thing, at the top of my profession! Where are the old values? – What about the promises? Not that I asked the questions willingly. But voices from the past, my ideals always, bogged down upon the fairy-tale! Let me be frank, I'm not complaining – I am complaining – I'd like to know, one way or the other that there is or is not, something more than the momentary pleasure . . . My very last try, or I'm afraid I must end it all and find my feet, Anastasia . . . I'm saying your eyes are blue, your hair is long, your skin is whiter than ever I was told.

ANASTASIA's *hand sloping towards the urn. Without looking up,* JAMES *puts his hand inside his jacket, withdraws a knife.* ANASTASIA *is still.*

(*Quietly.*) I was hoping, by your presence, that my hidden real beautiful self would, yeh know, show itself. I'm very beautiful, yeh know, but it's in hiding or something. And I'd like to feel it's twinge once more . . . A try?

ANASTASIA (*almost inaudible with fear*). No.

JAMES. We're alone.

ANASTASIA. No.

JAMES. And could start here, the two of us.

ANASTASIA. I must go now.

Slowly, fearfully, she starts to walk away. JAMES, motionless knife in hand.

JAMES. Come 'ere a minute . . . Come 'ere a minute.

Suddenly she dashes off.
A moment's pause and he is dashing after her.
ROSIE enters hauling a cylinder of gas.

ROSIE. James! James! I've rented the most secluded little cabin.

JAMES (*rounds on her*). Strumpet, slut, whore, Rosie!

He exits.

ROSIE. I only wanted to tell you where the cabin is. (*Delayed action.*) Pimp, ponce, Jame-Jame! (*Then tearfully.*) I'll get you, Jame-Jame . . .

ROSIE is collecting her cylinder of gas. Suddenly she freezes. EDMUND is entering. He is a handsome, confident young man in his early twenties. He is very innocent, romantic and charming. He wears a Robin Hood hat with a feather, an antique military tunic, jeans, high boots, a sword and a water-flask at his side.

He alters his course and exits without seeing her.

'Feathers'! What an escape! I was sure he would nab me. A Monster! Strong looking. Striking. My heart, if he had caught me! Or is he playing King Cagey? He wouldn't just ignore me?

She collects her cylinder of gas and exits, following him.

(*Tentatively.*) Hello there! . . . Hello there!

Scene Three

Another part of the forest.

ANASTASIA's *urn placed conspicuously on the ground.* ANASTASIA *enters tearfully. She sees the urn and hurries towards it joyfully. Her hand on the urn, and simultaneously* JAMES *steps out from behind a tree, triumphantly. He has his knife in one hand: he takes her hand and she appears submissive as he starts to lead her away. She stops. He looks at her suspiciously. Suddenly, she starts to scream, which he has not anticipated.* JAMES *in consternation.*

JAMES. Shush! shush!

EDMUND (*off*). Hullo-a! Hullo-a!

JAMES. 'Feathers'! – 'Feathers'!

EDMUND (*off*). Hullo-a! –

ROSIE (*off*). Hello there! –

JAMES. Shush, please shush!

In the struggle ANASTASIA *cuts her finger on* JAMES' *knife. She holds up her injured finger and faints.* EDMUND *enters background, criss-crossing through the trees, searching for the source of the screams.* JAMES *watching* EDMUND *working his way closer.*

EDMUND. Hullo-a! . . . Hullo-a! . . .

JAMES. But don't I know those features?

There is not time to carry off ANASTASIA; JAMES *hides behind a tree or climbs up into the tree.*

EDMUND. Hullo-a!

ROSIE (*entering background*). Hello there!

Through the scene ROSIE *works her way forward gradually, hauling cylinder of gas.*

EDMUND *finds* ANASTASIA. *for a moment he fears the worst. He revives her with a kiss. They look at each other in wonder.*

EDMUND. . . . But who are you?

ANASTASIA. Anastasia.

EDMUND. Anastasia!

ANASTASIA. And your eyes, green!

EDMUND. Anastasia!

ANASTASIA. Can it be?

EDMUND. Edmund is my name.

ANASTASIA. Edmund!

EDMUND. Anastasia! . . . But the way I found you here? Your hand: Is it not a knife wound?

ANASTASIA. From the blade of a dark horse who lay in wait, his red eye rolling in a starvation he claimed I could fill. How you must have come in the nick of time!

EDMUND. But what if beast still lurks here, hiding in the thickets. (*He has a look around.*)

ANASTASIA. Would he dare now that you are here.

EDMUND. Nevertheless. (*Wisely.*) I begin to learn a thing or two in travelling, you know.

ANASTASIA. And I told him how you wandered in the caves of my soul.

EDMUND. Yes?

ANASTASIA. But he closed his ears with monkey sounds.

EDMUND. And then?

ANASTASIA. We struggled.

EDMUND. He did not – ?

ANASTASIA. No.

EDMUND. Twas good, twas good, twas good, indeed, for I've been told that in the woe of such an act, the brightest gold of female spirit turns to brass contaminate.

ANASTASIA. And your voice a poet's.

EDMUND. All changed.

ANASTASIA *nods*.

EDMUND. Changed utterly . . . So now I must find two men. But let me bind this wicked wound. (*He binds her hand with his cravat.*)

ANASTASIA. You came in search of a man?

EDMUND. My brother James who has been long lost. Of his appearance my memory is vague for he still had years to grow a man when he left home. And through thrice nine lands I've wandered, being misued and mocked by words I did not understand. Once I journeyed North to find there was a James, but long gone 'poling'? wanderlusted South. And to a land down under where they told me of a last-remembered prisoned James, accused of rifling 'boxes' of the poor and convicted of the same offence 'gainst Convent postulants.

ANASTASIA (*uncomprehending wonder*). Oh.

EDMUND. In a vineless place there lived a drunkard James. In another and another, a pretender and imposter who'd present to me assuméd christian name and face, two pots of legacy-expectancy for eyes.

ANASTASIA. Oh.

EDMUND. And even in that parish last of all, where the aura was forbearance and the tenor fortitude, and I thought, at last, this is the end, for those attributes would compliment the standards of my brother: There I did, with galloping optimism of results, ignore the minor signposts, and straightaway the very top did go to his most serene the smiling red-haired bishop. His rosy ruby ring I kissed – And gold crozier as well – They well set off his smock and hat, a most imposing cleric's drag! But scarce my genuflecting ritual was done and I had spoken of my quest, than at mention of the name of James, the red-haired bishop's smiling face went tighting into august ire, his holy head did copper-beach. And summoned by the bells that pealed emergency in Roman morse, two military P.P.s arrived to lead me to the shore and feed me to an oarless boat. And here I am.

ANASTASIA. My poor brave love.

EDMUND. But when we meet the noble evidence of James will show as candle does when lighted under tinder bush.

JAMES, *sloping away, steps on a twig – or he nearly falls out of the tree.*

ANASTASIA. Oh, what was that?

They are poised listening, EDMUND *hand on sword.*

EDMUND. A crow.

ANASTASIA. A crow?

EDMUND. The only bird I loathe!

Other twigs snapping.

ANASTASIA. And that!

EDMUND. And that! –

ROSIE (*approaching, steps on a twig, calls softly*). Hello there! –

ANASTASIA. And that! –

ROSIE *has just seen* EDMUND *and she is pleased with herself.* (*Neither* EDMUND *nor* ANASTASIA *see her.*) *Then her terror as* EDMUND *speaks angrily, drawing his sword.*

EDMUND (*drawing sword*). Tis the bane! No loathed crow could make such noise!

ROSIE *bolts for it. The noise she makes running through the trees confuses* EDMUND *and he alters his course to follow her.*

He thinks to escape! Now I shall accomplish half the remainder of my mission!

ANASTASIA *watches* EDMUND *rush off, admiring his manly courage and anger.*

JAMES *returns and grabs her – or he drops off the tree and lands beside her.*

JAMES. Didn't want to meet you, puppy-fat, did I? Had sworn never-more.

ANASTASIA. Ed–

JAMES (*twisting her arm*). Go on, try shouting again now, go on.

He tears a piece of cloth off her dress and throws it on the path opposite the one he intends to take.

ANASTASIA. Edmund will find me.

JAMES (*bitterly*). Edmund. I should have known. Well, it only makes it worse who he is!

ANASTASIA. Where are you taking me?

JAMES. I'll find a place. This time I leave no trail.

EDMUND *is returning.* JAMES *hurries off with* ANASTASIA.

EDMUND. He escaped this time, but my promise to thrash him will be . . . Anastasia? (*Calls.*) Anastasia, where are you?

ROSIE *enters background, ready to run again, a mixture of terror and delight, breathing heavily.* ROSIE *comes forward cautiously.*

ROSIE. Hello there!

EDMUND. Anastasiaaa!

ROSIE. Hello there!

EDMUND (*to himself*). If needs be I shall do that villain in, you know?

ROSIE (*striking whore's pose*). Can I help you?

EDMUND (*striding past* ROSIE *to pick up the piece of cloth torn off* ANASTASIA's *dress*). Ah! God directs my steps. (*He is about to exit.*)

ROSIE (*angry at being ignored*). Whom do you bloody-well think you're following, Feathers?

EDMUND *turns about and draws his sword.* ROSIE, *sinks to her knees, trying to protect her head and ribs with her arms. Then* EDMUND *strides past her and kills a snake.*

EDMUND. Oh, that you were the villain, snake!

ROSIE *faints,* EDMUND *revives her, slapping her hands.*

Maybe with her wits a little fostered she could help me.

ROSIE. Oh my love, I love you so much.

EDMUND. There is beauty in the blue truth of your eye and your eye is not light, I cannot be thine.

ROSIE. It was just a salutation.

EDMUND. And you are fairer than anyone knows at a second glance.

ROSIE. Forget it.

EDMUND. Someone can help you.

ROSIE. Little Jesus.

EDMUND. He has graced you with sensitivity.

ROSIE (*loudly, cynically*). And my legs! My legs! You noticed my feelings, but not bad, are they? (*She has pulled up her skirt.*) What's your game?

EDMUND. I had hoped for information of the maiden Anastasia.

ROSIE. What's she got to do with it?

EDMUND. You know her?

ROSIE. The one with the jug on her head?

EDMUND. You know her!

ROSIE. I was looking for a cylinder of gas for the cabin.

EDMUND. Yes, yes – yes?

ROSIE. She gave me directions, that's all.

EDMUND. She is fair, she is lovely.

ROSIE. She's a wet kid, she knows nothing!

EDMUND. She is –

ROSIE. Nothing! (ROSIE *is quietly triumphant at killing the subject.*)

EDMUND (*moving off*). She cannot help me.

ROSIE. Hold on! I mean, people get the wrong idea if we girls make too much of other girls, get me? Better to stick to the traditional stuff: meeow! Okay?

EDMUND (*does not understand*). Yes.

ROSIE (*watching his face*). I like your boots . . . And your
water-flask. Oh, and ostrich, is it? Very nice. (EDMUND *feels
flattered*.) Hmm? I mean, you didn't come here trailing the
kid now, did you?

EDMUND. But our paths have been converging since the
exordium.

ROSIE. The things you boys say to me! Honestly! The way you
boys will cling to the crap! Man is a fool, they say. Me now, I
shed tears and crap, all in one go; I don't get involved, not
any more, my name is Rosie, and I feel the better for it . . .
You don't believe me? Well, alright, I confess. One single
dream remaining. But adult, practical and possible. For I have
dreamed, you see, that someone someday'd come along and
turn my working blanket into a magic carpet. Away! Just
once will be enough . . . (*She smiles at him.*) My real name is
Mary Rose. Unsolicited, persons started to call me Rosie.

EDMUND. Then I shall call you Mary Rose.

ROSIE. Do you kiss?

EDMUND. Mary Rose –

ROSIE. You don't have to get involved –

EDMUND. But the maiden Anastasia.

ROSIE. She'd be no use to you! Tck! He doesn't understand.

EDMUND (*wisely*). Oh, I know a thing or two.

ROSIE. Yeh? . . . I'm beginning to see you're pretty sharp
alright. And maybe my little dream remaining is near
fulfilment. I'll help you.

EDMUND. I'll pay you.

ROSIE *flicks out her hand for him to kiss it.*

ROSIE. For a start.

EDMUND. Mary Rose –

ROSIE. Kiss my hand –

EDMUND. Believe you must –

ROSIE. It's just a hand –

EDMUND. That fidelity's single breach –

ROSIE. You saved my life –

EDMUND. Would me impossible make for Anastasia.

ROSIE. My platonic poxy hand, for little Jesus' sake!

As he kisses her hand.

Got him . . . Now, what's your game?

EDMUND. I am now in search of three.

ROSIE. And the second you seek?

EDMUND. A villain.

ROSIE. Yes James, and – (*Her hand to her mouth, fears she has made a slip.*)

EDMUND. You know James? The third I seek is James!

ROSIE. Well, he's just a friend, a kind of sort of Bill.

EDMUND (*about to exit*). She cannot help me or herself.

ROSIE. I'll lead you to James!

He stops.

Well, you'll give him no more than a right good belting, right? (*Angrily.*) Well, the fact is, I need spectacles. What ammunition the ponce would make of that if he knew! And what ammunition for me if I'm forced to return and go my profession alone wearing spectacles!

EDMUND (*to himself*). This does not sound a likely James.

ROSIE. What? Well, do you know – Do-you-know! – that every single day in nineteen years he's thought of ditching me, leaving me? Do you know that? He would too, but he thinks I'd die without him.

EDMUND. And would you not?

ROSIE. No.

EDMUND. That's the pity.

ROSIE (*softly*). I know. (*Shakes off the sadness.*) No need for your jaws to grow long with sincerity about it!

EDMUND. But what are his accomplishments?

ROSIE. His mother played piano.

EDMUND. What?!

ROSIE. And do you know that, in spite of all, I appear to cater for his every whim? Do you know that? But the fact that I appear to cater for his every whim means nothing. The truth is in the opposite, they say. This catering lark is just a dreary pastime, a traditional common-or-garden aspect in the routine of the female disposition, they say. I'll lead you to him. Spiritually we have nothing. Except the poxy habit of time. And ask myself to recall when his intimacies meant other than a client's, and my memory only shrugs and shakes its head. Granted, I've grown accustomed to being used. But by my clientele. Well, c'est la vie, they pays their money and vaya con Dios. But that my gift of sex to James is taken as a bas-relief and nothing more! It's therapy, they say. Nevertheless, an unkind cut. God knows it is. (*Winces.*) And little Jesus.

EDMUND (*his mother*). Played piano?

ROSIE. Yes! My daddy and my uncle Joe were right: What do I know of the ponce!

EDMUND. Concert?

ROSIE. Exactly! Concert? Honky-tonk? One hand?

They exit with cylinder of gas.

Scene Four

A log cabin in the forest. (For this scene the cabin retains its fourth wall: we do not see ANASTASIA.*)* JAMES *comes out of cabin. He calls back.*

JAMES. But latent sexuality can thicken the air unduly. So, to come to the point I'm coming to, I'm not saying we should preclude irrevocably – irrevocably what could become pleasure at some later date. If such should be your wont, yeh know. Or mine. (*To himself.*) A stroke of luck finding this place alright. Secluded. Safe. That stupid dumb-cluck Rosie's probably rented a little cabin right in among the dirty natives.

ROSIE (*off*). This way! The thing is he mightn't be at home.

JAMES, *in consternation, in and out of the cabin, and in again.*

ROSIE *and* EDMUND *entering.*

(*Points to the cabin.*) Isn't it nice. (*Calls.*) James! He's not at home. But let me show you what it's like inside.

JAMES *comes out of the cabin. Trying to conceal his fear, holding the door closed behind him. He is now wearing a pair of dark glasses.* ROSIE's *surprise and disappointment. She goes forward.*

How did you find it?

JAMES. Aw Jesus! (*Quietly.*) Get the bastard out of here.

ROSIE. Stall it, relax, the kid's a mug.

JAMES. Aw Jesus! (*Loudly.*) Where have you been, madam?

ROSIE. It's okay, we misjudged him.

JAMES (*loudly*). What have you been doing, madam?

ROSIE. On the way here he told me he's looking for his brother or something.

JAMES (*loudly*). I hope you're not deaf, madam!

ROSIE (*loudly, angrily*). I-was-getting-a-cylinder-of-gas! (*Motioning* EDMUND *to join them*.) This is James; James, this is — Oh, what's your name?

EDMUND. My name is Edmund —

JAMES (*ignores* EDMUND's *hand*). I'll teach you to talk to strangers!

ROSIE (*angrily*). I said I've checked him out!

JAMES. Wait till I get you inside, madam!

ROSIE. What's the big deal for? Well this is good, this is rich, this is really bingo! He, Edmund! — Him, Edmund! — That! — has me out on the bye-ways every night 'cept Mondays, and now he's asking what I was doing.

JAMES. You lousy whore of a tell-tale, Rosie!

His hand raised to strike ROSIE, EDMUND *grabs his hand and yanks him about.* JAMES' *dark glasses fall off.* EDMUND's *and* JAMES' *heads close together, looking into each others' eyes.* EDMUND *beginning to look troubled.* JAMES *growing cocky, fancying himself, seeing* EDMUND's *distress. Their hands continue, locked together, straining with each other.*

EDMUND. Quickly, who are you?

ROSIE. Croak him, Edmund!

JAMES (*cockily to* ROSIE). Who's the gomey?

ROSIE. Break his arm off.

JAMES. Who's the buffer with the archaic gimmick?

EDMUND. It were better that you told me.

JAMES. A pop-poet!

EDMUND. Or I shall — I shall break your arm off!

ROSIE. Do! Do!

JAMES. Are you able? Are you able? Alrighty! Let's see. Come on, good old devil.

The contest begins in earnest, the effort, forcing them into intricate bodily contortions. JAMES is delighted, showing slightly to advantage.

ROSIE (*to* EDMUND). Get him in the cobblers, Edmund. (*Tugging at* JAMES, *feigning concern for* JAMES.) Don't, James, he'll hurt you.

JAMES. I'm in control now.

ROSIE. He'll break your arm off.

JAMES. Back, madam! Don't weaken me. I've got the bastard now.

EDMUND *increases his effort and* JAMES *is eventually forced to submit.*

EDMUND. Do you still challenge?

JAMES. I do! I do!

EDMUND. Do you still?

JAMES. I yi – yi – yi do! . . . You that's doing all the challenging!

EDMUND. Still challenge?

JAMES. I yi – yi – yi – yi! – No! No! I don't!

EDMUND *releases him.* JAMES *trots away, stops.*

I do! I do!

JAMES *turns to run away again, trips, falls.*

EDMUND (*offering his hand*). My name is –

JAMES. Don't want to know you, or anything to do with you! (*Stands.*) Now! But there will be another time. (*To* ROSIE.) And, you! Inside! – Home! – At once!

ROSIE (*pitying* EDMUND *who looks upset*). Aaaaa!

JAMES. At once!

ROSIE *is moving towards the cabin when* JAMES *remembers that* ANASTASIA *is in there.*

Just a moment, madam!

ROSIE *obeys, waits for instructions.* JAMES *stuck for a reason to give her.*

Nevertheless . . . So, yeh know, but, well! Well, I would have won only for you! You weakened me!

ROSIE. Aaa, he isn't even half wide, James, he's nice.

EDMUND (*to himself*). Something's gone awry. All others in his category did frantically claim relationship with guile. And his mother played piano.

ROSIE. Aa, what's troubling you, Edmund?

JAMES (*nervously*). Nothing troubling me – nothing troubling me.

EDMUND. A favour?

JAMES. A ruse.

ROSIE. Anything.

JAMES. King Cagey.

EDMUND. I ask it simply: what is your surname?

ROSIE. Well, like, mine is still sort of different, but his is –

JAMES. Let me answer that very impertinent personal question (*To* ROSIE.) You stall your jills. (*To* EDMUND.) Jones.

EDMUND (*doubtfully*). Your surname?

JAMES. That's what I said.

EDMUND. What?

JAMES. Well, what's yours?

EDMUND. . . . Oh, I have learned a thing or two in travelling, you know.

JAMES. I've got a trick or two myself —

EDMUND. I know a thing or two —

JAMES. I've got a trick or two —

EDMUND. And I've evolved a formula for 'vincing truth!

> JAMES *crouches suddenly, poised, waiting for this next contest. They start to circle each other. Then suddenly.*

> Grandfather's old apple tree?

JAMES. N-N-Name of a pub!

EDMUND. No — In the garden.

JAMES. On the river the one I know!

EDMUND. Home, James?

JAMES. And don't spare the horses!

EDMUND. Bringing in the sheaves?

JAMES. Every other cowboy picture!

EDMUND (*growing dismayed*). Teddy-bear with one ear is living in the attic.

JAMES. Teddy Bear is a retired boxer!

> JAMES *is giggling nervously, feeling he has won.*

EDMUND (*dismayed*). . . . Bapu.

> JAMES' *giggling triumph changing to puzzlement. Then feigning casualness.*

JAMES. Ah . . . bapu?

EDMUND (*still with eyes cast down*). Twas Jameses charming infant word when asking for an apple.

The shadow of a memory on JAMES' face, his vigilance relaxing, his stance wilting and EDMUND is in; JAMES frustrated.

Had you a very unhappy childhood, where were you born?

JAMES. I – yi – yi – yi – Which of them?

EDMUND. Place of birth.

JAMES. I – yi – yi – yi – In a ball-alley! I was born in a –

EDMUND. Your parents?

JAMES. Were called Jones too!

EDMUND. I mean, sir –

JAMES. They were awful! – They were awful! – They were – Stop!

EDMUND is watching him with interest. He trots away from EDMUND.

(*Quietly.*) You'd better go home, sonny, leave us alone, sonny, go 'way, go home, people are dying.

EDMUND. I will find my brother first.

JAMES. Not here.

EDMUND. I have travelled far and wide –

JAMES. Don't want to know.

EDMUND. I don't believe you are a wicked man, James Jones –

JAMES (*feebly*). No baits, don't throw any baits.

EDMUND. You would think that all the Jameses in the world accursed, but I know better. I shall always know better.

Pause. The three of them motionless. JAMES trying to maintain a hard expression. He turns his back. ROSIE comes out of her stillness, a girlish glow about her.

ROSIE. Let's . . . Let's all do something! Let's all go somewhere. I know! The pub! A few drinks! And you can continue your search on the way, Edmund.

EDMUND *looks at* JAMES.

Yes, James, the three of us! Do let's!

JAMES *nods, motioning them to go on ahead of him. ROSIE and EDMUND exit. JAMES turns about. His face easing into a weary softness.*

JAMES. 'Bapu' . . . Ah, this won't last, this feeling won't. It's all treachery.

After a moment he breaks into a weary trot and exits following EDMUND and ROSIE.

Scene Five

Night. The cabin.

ROSIE, EDMUND *and* JAMES *enter, approaching the cabin. ROSIE and JAMES are drunk. ROSIE has a bottle of gin. They are singing and dancing their way home. EDMUND is enjoying himself, his youthful exuberance encouraging him to complement some of* ROSIE's *movements – though he does not quite partner her.*

And though JAMES is drunk, smiling, nodding encouragingly, bringing up the rear, he is too watchful, the smile too fixed, the nodding too benign. And he is carrying EDMUND's sword, ostensibly to allow EDMUND greater freedom of movement. Through the song he perhaps slips away from them, races into the cabin and hides the sword under the bed.

*It is mainly ROSIE who does the singing; the others
complement.*

ROSIE (*singing*).

> Life's no bucking bron-co!
> How's your uncle's bald head?
> Life is no dud, oh no!
> Life is so good, yeah, yeah!

> Come on, you old pair of pub-crawling bums! Let's have a
> party!

> Life's no bucking bron-co! – Where's James?
> Let go the bloody handlebars!
> Up she flew-wuw, touché!
> Life's a good screw, yeah-yeah!

*The lights come up on the cabin as they enter. There is a
main room which contains a few simple chairs, a table and a
bed. And separated from this by a locked door is a small
room on an elevated level. In the small room we see
ANASTASIA gagged and bound to a chair. She remains thus
throughout the scene.*

EDMUND. How she (ANASTASIA) would enjoy this evening!

JAMES. Glasses, Rosie!

ROSIE. Coming up, James!

JAMES. Not bad, is she? Getting old now, but not bad, is she?

EDMUND. I have great admiration for Mary Rose.

JAMES. Hear that, Rose?

ROSIE. Yep!

JAMES (*confidentially to* EDMUND). You wouldn't think it,
but she's not a whore at all, yeh know. And she was very well
educated, her father a judge and her Uncle Joe a bishop. So, I
could have done worse, hmm?

EDMUND. And her hospitality.

JAMES. Yes, her hospitality – but I've done pretty well for myself when you think of it another way. I didn't make many mistakes and I –

EDMUND. And her vigour.

JAMES. Yes, yes, her vigour, her figure, but *I*, all-in-all, did alright, and I must say I –

EDMUND. The pith of vigour.

JAMES (EDMUND's *innocence hurting him. Harshly*). Yes – yes, randy, boy, randy!

EDMUND (*smiling*). Yes.

JAMES *is sulking.*
ROSIE *is bringing glasses to the table.*

ROSIE. Come on, Edmund, sit down. (*Quietly.*) Don't depress him, noo, shh! (*Loudly.*) And I'll buy you a leather jock-strap trimmed with sequins tomorrow! (*Quietly.*) Stay the night. (*Loudly.*) God, that last place we were in, James, bored the knickers off me! (JAMES *sighs.*) Now, Edmund, you're not going to keep drinking water all night, you're going to have your first gin.

JAMES (*sharply*). The kid's a natural non-drinker! If he's a water-baby, he's a water-baby!

ROSIE, *surprised at this protective attitude.*

Oh, it's got nothing to do with me.

EDMUND. I should like to attempt one gin, everyone appeared so happy at the inn. And I should not like to appear an outsider.

EDMUND *raises his glass apprehensively, self-consciously. All eyes on him. He hesitates, drinks, coughs, and is pleased with the experiment.*

Cheers! (*They laugh.*) What convivial hosts! (*Looks towards small room.*) But will we not awaken the children.

JAMES (*motions him to bend closer*). Come here, I'll tell you about that. Rosie?

ROSIE *nods in pre-concurrence.*

Now, I wouldn't give any woman a baby. I would be afraid to give any woman a baby, Edmund. Once a woman has a baby she's first-rate happy then. And man isn't so so-so-so, yeh know, anymore. (*For her confirmation.*) Rosie?

ROSIE. Man is only a tool, Edmund.

EDMUND. But what is wrong with making someone happy?

JAMES. And what about me?

EDMUND. You want to have a baby?

JAMES. Aw Jesus! – Aw, Edmund! Don't be silly. He doesn't understand –

ROSIE. That's what I've been saying. But it's nice.

EDMUND. I understand.

JAMES. What?

EDMUND. Giving happiness, gives one pleasure. In youth I was told, you can't do –

JAMES. You can't do a good thing too often! Rosie?

JAMES *and* ROSIE *laugh bawdily.* EDMUND *smiling innocently.*

(*Laughing scornfully.*) He doesn't get it! (*Continues laughing, growing frustrated.*) He doesn't get it, he doesn't get it! – I don't get it now! – What does it matter? – Hate smelly babies! – Hate them!

Silence.

ROSIE *offers to top up* EDMUND's *glass.* EDMUND *refuses.*

(*Irritably.*) Why not?

EDMUND. Its merit I recognise but will remain with the twofold elevation of the one: savour and the virtue of its moderation.

Another silence.

JAMES. Well, can you sing?

EDMUND. I can.

JAMES. Will you?

EDMUND. I will.

JAMES *and* ROSIE *settle themselves anticipating something pleasant.* EDMUND *sings the first line 'Down in the forest' and delivers the remainder in wonder.*

Down in the forest . . . I saw her. And my being fed to regeneration. And the meaning of everything became clear and unimportant. And once I closed my eyes to trap the angel self within me, but all of me had fused to become one sensitive eye, drinking in God, or was I radiating Him? or was I Him?

JAMES. Lovely! —

ROSIE. Bravo! —

EDMUND. Not finished. Then. (*He shivers.*) Down in the forest . . . I lay upon the fallen leaves, the only noise was dying hushed derision. And then the quietness of a smile, so strange and still, no sound to cheer the accomplishment of journey's end, for my mission was quite done. And then I lookéd up to see a crow alighting from a tree, to perch upon my breast. I wondered at his fearless apathetic eye more beadier than fish's fixed on mine, and I wondered at his mystery purpose: 'twas not good. The cakéd offal on his beak was grey, and then he ope'd it up to show the stiffened corpse of maggot for a tongue. I knew that birds are sometimes known in vagary to offer their own store to human kind, and so I thought I would accept, to please the crow for he was dark, his succulence, his relish, my disgust. And then I checked my mouth to find that it was shut as in paralysis. And then – O God! – my eyes I found were open with such tautness: they were gaping bulges wide. And though I would I could not race my fear towards liberating climax, to release me in a roar. And on and on the insult of my tightened lips I stared back, in the innocence of silent nightmare. And then he pecked; I was so young, and that was that.

Pause. EDMUND *smiling.*

ROSIE (*nervously*). I was very musical; once I could play –

JAMES. I was so young, I played it straight –

ROSIE (*as in a panic*). We played it straight, James, we played it straight, James –

JAMES. I was such a youth, I was such a child, I was such a baby for the fairytale –

ROSIE. All we did was try to live –

JAMES. Starting with the natural things –

ROSIE. Sing us a song, James –

JAMES. It's easy to sing –

ROSIE. It's easy to sing, James, sing us a song –

JAMES. Who's talking?

ROSIE. You are.

JAMES. It's easy to sing . . . What is the past?

ROSIE. A fairytale.

JAMES. Shut up. A broken promise. Wouldn't it be better to – I don't mean frighten the daylights out of babies – but to warn them a bit. Yeh know. A few rotten hints now and again and that.

ROSIE. Forearmed is –

JAMES. Shut up. You were about to say?

EDMUND. Mary Rose was speaking.

ROSIE. I'm finished.

JAMES (*to her*). What? – (*To him.*) What?

EDMUND. But was not the past golden, nevertheless?

JAMES. Yes – yes – yes, very golden nevertheless. What came after?

ROSIE. Sing us a song, James, tell us a story – Oh he has a lovely story, personal and subjective.

JAMES. Not personal! Only any old story! Now!

EDMUND. Do narrate, but I must anon be gone to continue my search for Anastasia.

JAMES. For who? (*He has forgotten all about her.*)

EDMUND. Anastasia.

ROSIE (*answering JAMES' puzzlement*). Anastasia!

JAMES (*finally remembers*). Yes, well, yes.

ROSIE. The story, James.

JAMES. What? –

EDMUND. The title.

JAMES. No title! –

ROSIE. Aaa do, aa doo, it's lovely.

JAMES. Not lovely! Now! Yeh know . . . Once upon a time there was a boy, as there was always and as there always will be, and he was given a dream, his life. His mother told him do not be naughty, who would be naughty, no one is naughty. And there would be a lovely girl for him one day, and she would have blue eyes and golden hair. His mother was very very beautiful and good. His father taught him honesty, to stand erect and be sincere and tell no lies, like every other person in the world, his brothers. And that on the stroke of twelve on his twenty-first birthday he would become a man, and he would not be afraid to have his appendix out, and he would get better and better and better. And the teachers too were saintly men and could answer all his questions. They told him of the good laws, and how bad laws could not work because they were bad. And sums, so as not to burden anybody with his ignorance in the years ahead, his life. And the books he read were filled with heroes; people lived happily, ugliness was sure to turn to beauty, and poor boys were better than rich boys because they were noble really, and they married the loveliest girl you ever saw, and she had blue eyes and golden hair. And the church told him of God, kind God and guardian angels. And how everyone is made just like God – even the little boy himself was. There was a devil but he was not alive; he was dead really. And the kindest stork you ever saw with a great red beak would take care of any works and pomps. And there were things called politicians for doing favours and seeing to things. Be a good citizen is all they asked and vote for us and we shall do the rest. And there was a king there for – that was not quite clear. But he was there, like in all the other stories. Not that anything would go wrong, but he was keeping an eye on things all the same. Not that anything could go wrong. He was there, probably, to make the boy's life his dream.

EDMUND. Bravo! Bravo! Exceeding lovely, James indeed!

JAMES. Not finished . . . Yes, everyone gave the little boy balloons, the most expensive balloons, already inflated, yellow, green, blue and red, the very best of colours, and they floated above him, nodding and bobbing, and lifting his feet clear off the ground so that he never had to walk a step anywhere. Until, one day, one of them burst, and it was the beautiful blue one. And he was not prepared for this. So, one day, he walked away into the forest forever.

ROSIE. And one by one the other balloons burst.

EDMUND. A naughty little boy.

JAMES. What?

EDMUND. For bursting his balloons.

JAMES. What! Does a little boy burst his own balloons?

EDMUND. If a naughty little boy he is. And then he tries to burst the balloons of good and mannered little boys.

JAMES. What! The very clots of people who gave them to him! What sort of monk are you?

EDMUND. Those clots of people got balloons too.

JAMES. And what happened to them? Burst! By the clots of people who gave them to them! So you'd imagine someone would learn something, wouldn't you?

ROSIE. I think –

JAMES. *You* think? *You* think? –

ROSIE. Yes, I think – I say they'll have to stop bursting sometime that's all!

JAMES. No, daftie! No, madam! They'll have to stop giving them out! That's all! Now! – (*To* EDMUND.) Yes?

EDMUND. What befell the little boy in the end?

JAMES. Died.

EDMUND. Without a –

JAMES. No balloons, died, nothing, and he lived happily ever after.

ROSIE. What about a little music?

ROSIE *goes to the door of the small room and finds it locked. She tugs at the handle.* JAMES *is unperturbed by her action.*

(*To herself.*) This door is locked.

EDMUND. Your story was well told.

JAMES. I'm a queer shot. I'm very well educated too, but invariably I do my moronic bit when I'm annoyed. We're annoyed see, so we don't like talking nice. Rosie? (*For her confirmation.*)

ROSIE (*tugging at door handle*). You can say that for bloody sure.

JAMES. I used to talk nice all the time. When I'm in the driver's seat I still occasionally talk nice. Also, occasionally, when I'm chatting up crumpet. (*Explaining.*) Charvers.

ROSIE (*abandoning the door*). That door is locked.

JAMES. And most women are thick, so you talk nice to them. The thicker they are, the nicer you talk. I tried a lot of women, didn't I. Rosie?

ROSIE. Yep.

JAMES. That's in case you'd think. And especially in the initial chatting-up stakes you enunciate. But while you're talking nice, because they are so thick, before you know what's happening, they've got you, a nice guy, turned into a creeping Jesus, until you've got so low you're Mephistopheles. For instance, I noticed Rosie here giving you the wink.

EDMUND. But –

JAMES. No – no, no need to rebut, I don't mind. I'm in the driver's seat as it happens. But you don't understand that neither. So, to come to the point I'm coming to: if one loves, one should be in love. Do you see what I mean?

ROSIE. If one loves one should be in love, James. Simple alive.

JAMES. No need to embellish. I'll make a statement. I am in love. Hmm? (*Sing-songing, drunkenly, childishly.*) I am in love! – Free as a bird! – The birds are my friends! I am going to soar, to soar, to soar, to fly, on my very last try, my very last try! Caw, caw, caw! I'm a red sky at night, I have found my dream, I will never wake up, my dream – my dream, my future at last!

ROSIE (*laughing, starting on a high note and down the scale*). If-I-don't-win-him-soon-how-can-my-love-be-like-a-rose!

JAMES (*embarrassed*). Haw-haw, dream, Edmund! Rosie, haw, love! (*Then, wary, anticipating* EDMUND.) Yes?

EDMUND. You are making your last try here?

JAMES. What? Not necessarily in this room. I mean – What do you mean, exactly, 'here'? I promise you I didn't want to try again. Rosie?

ROSIE. On the contrary.

JAMES. Can't you take a simple statement? And there's been a bastard following me about and, no matter who he is, if I catch up on him, I'll – Well, he'd better watch his P's and Q's. Yes?

EDMUND. This last time you are trying – Mary Rose, of course?

JAMES. Mary Rose! Mary Rose! . . . What are you looking at my eye for? I happen to be genuinely fond of old Rosie – Mary Rose. Pretty fond of her.

He gives a hug and a little kiss to ROSIE.

So, yeh know, you have a nice bright night outside for your search.

He goes out of the cabin. Leaving the door open for EDMUND.

EDMUND (*bows to* ROSIE). Thank you.

ROSIE. He's sobered up.

EDMUND. Yes.

ROSIE. Another time.

EDMUND. Yes.

She purses her lips for him to kiss her.

Mary Rose –

ROSIE ⎫ Just my cheek then – just my cheek –
EDMUND ⎭ Believe you must that fidelity's single breach –

ROSIE. For God's sake, my platonic poxy cheek!

As EDMUND *kisses her on the cheek.*

Got him! Round two.

EDMUND *goes out of the cabin.*

Third and final round coming up.

ROSIE *goes to bed.*

JAMES *sees* EDMUND *coming out of the cabin and he races across the stage to hide. Then, thinking that* EDMUND *has gone,* JAMES *is racing back to the cabin, gleefully, and has passed* EDMUND *before he realises* EDMUND's *presence. He returns to* EDMUND *wearily.*

JAMES. Oh yeh?

EDMUND. Curiously, your story reminds me of the parting-day my brother, coincidentally a James, left home.

JAMES. Oh yeh?

EDMUND. And from unexchangéd glances it was plain, that twixt my ma and he, all was not well.

JAMES. Oh yeh?

EDMUND. The unshed tears and unspoke words gave an aura to our home of deploration.

JAMES. Oh yeh?

EDMUND. And though both ma and da most earnestly declared that James a saint some day would be, my languishment's remained.

JAMES. Come to the point.

EDMUND. Well, it may be so that no successful saint has James become, or even lowly living cherubim, but so much more would we love him if I could bring him home.

JAMES. To our mountains.

EDMUND. And to vales.

JAMES. Jesus kid!

EDMUND. To love.

JAMES. To dress him up in hope again?

EDMUND. He need not be ashamed.

JAMES. For a new batch of balloons for a new batch of pins?

EDMUND. James –

JAMES. Jee-sus kid! Did it not occur to you that this James character – whoever he might be – might be choking with their home-made love and mem-o-ries?

EDMUND. My brother James is –

JAMES. Did it never strike you pink that he might really be a mean-un?

EDMUND. James –

JAMES. Then you look out! Cause twill strike you blind and strike you dumb when you find out, suddenlike, he is no funny man and not a fool. That he's a volunteer for dirty deeds, that he's mightily proud of getting worse, that he aims to hit rock-bottom, for his basis. Now, if you'll take my advice you'll go home, and tell those bringing-in-the-sheafers that you met the man who has escaped. He's not their victim anymore. You tell them that.

EDMUND. But, James, you have misunderstood.

JAMES. No-no-no-no now, baby! Don't you try to sweetheart me again. We've had that bit.

EDMUND. But, James —

JAMES. And let's have done with the innocent shit. See, I'm a believer in honest, open ignorance, not innocence. Don't you confuse the two like the hypocrites like to do. They manured our honest open ignorance on moral crap and fairy snow, then sent us out as innocents to chew the ears off any man, wife, stranger, friend, and kick their hearts to death in the name of Jesus Christ or Santa Claus to boot. (*To himself.*) Till you don't know where you are or what you are or —

EDMUND } James, you are my —
JAMES   } Who are you! I don't know who I am but I'm not going to be no sunlamplit brother of anyone!

EDMUND *opens his mouth to speak.*

Jesus, he will not listen to me!

EDMUND *opens his mouth.*

No! Look, leave me alone, I'm tired, I've been on the go! (*A plead.*) Rock-bottom for my basis, what's wrong with that? I must get my feet on the ground, Edmund. My mind is such a coloured kite, Edmund. I've got so much crap to unload, you would not believe! It's a simple case of honest terra firma or caput for me. Do you dig?

EDMUND *nods.*

You're codding me now?

EDMUND *shakes his head.*

And I'm such a weary little dear. Isn't that honest of me?

EDMUND *nods.*

Well, let's split for now and hit for bunkeroonysville. Hmm?

EDMUND *looks sad.* JAMES *moves away a little. Stops.*

. . . I need my kip, Edmund. (*Sighs, returns wearily to*
EDMUND.)

Yeh?

EDMUND. I have a message for my brother.

JAMES. That's as maybe. Yeh?

EDMUND. Granddaddy died.

JAMES. Oh yeh?

EDMUND. Grandmammy outlasted him by seven minutes.

JAMES. Oh yeh.

EDMUND. Father died.

JAMES. Oh yeh?

EDMUND. Mother is dead . . . Ma is dead.

JAMES. Oh yeh?

EDMUND. She said to tell James she forgave him. Loved him.
She was old and yellow and withered and grey, her hands
worn with care when she died. Even the King was there, his
last respects to pay. But it was you she wanted to hear say
you loved her.

JAMES. He die?

EDMUND. What?

JAMES (*harshly*). The King – the King!

EDMUND. He did.

JAMES. Good.

EDMUND. Say it to the night, James.

JAMES (*quietly*). You won't give up, will you?

EDMUND. She will hear you.

JAMES. That crow will come and peck the bubbles of your eyes.

EDMUND. You can feel her in the night, listening, waiting.

JAMES. Look, I'm sure you had a nice mother, kid, you know.

EDMUND. You can say that sincerely, without prevarication?

JAMES (*prevaricating*). Ah-hmm? – Yeh.

EDMUND. Perhaps I have been on another erring tack. I'll continue my search for Anastasia.

EDMUND *salutes and exits.*

JAMES *considers calling* EDMUND *back and relinquishing* ANASTASIA. *He changes his mind. He trots into the cabin.* ROSIE *is asleep. He gets* EDMUND's *sword from under the bed and deliberately nicks his finger with the point. He smears his blood on the blade. He unlocks the door of the little room and goes in to* ANASTASIA. *He holds the blood-stained sword under her nose.*

JAMES. He's dead!

He thrusts the sword into the floor so that it stands upright.

The lights fade.

Scene Six

Moonlight. JAMES *is sitting outside the cabin waiting-up for cock-crow; occasionally glances back at the cabin where he has left* ANASTASIA.

JAMES (*trying to be poetic*). Ah, the moon! . . . The moon, the moon, that . . . orb! That . . . Come on, old cock, crow! A nice early crow this morning . . . That . . . orb! Crow, just once, good cock, and I will be hers and she, mine, our lives to begin together, forever: What a lovely little signal she chose! . . . Crow!

He dozes, wakes with a start, flicking his hand across his forehead.

Nickerdehpazzee! Dead hand so mottled, brown so worn with care! I'll nail you witch! I'll nail you! . . . But how? Speak well of them that persecute you. Who said that? The cunning of it. Some bury them with a smile and a tear, some with a prayer and a nail . . . I'll try. (*Braces himself, begins with an effort.*) God gave me a wonderful mammy, her memory will never grow old, her smile was – (*Angrily.*) Aw, yes – yes, her memory, heart, smile, head, hands, promises! . . . What am I doing here, mooning? I swore never more. Why, properly pruned of the dead wood I could be almost anything . . . Who said that? . . . That poxy-looking prick of an orb up there! Just another American ad now! . . . (*Wearily, dozing.*) Aw, but when that cocky chap crows, just once . . . (*Groans.*) Jimmy . . . Yeh know . . . (*He falls asleep.*)

Morning lights the cabin.

We can now see into the cabin. The chair that ANASTASIA was bound to in the small room is vacant. The sword remains upright stuck in the floor, the back of the chair up against it, and lengths of rope are strewn on the floor. The suggestion is that ANASTASIA manoeuvred the chair into this position and freed herself. There is no sign of ANASTASIA. (She is hiding in the room but we do not see her.)

ROSIE gets out of bed, yawning, looks about for JAMES; old slippers, an old dressing gown. She comes out of the cabin speaking in her morning baby voice.

ROSIE. My Jamie sity (*sitting*) upy all nighty. Why, Jame-Jame?

JAMES (*awakes*). Ah?!

ROSIE. Naughty, Jamie, catchy coldy.

JAMES (*absently*). The bastard cock, why doesn't he crow?

ROSIE *laughs, not understanding, and bends to kiss him. He pushes her away.*

ROSIE. Not nicey. And you behaved so well last nighty. Such a lovely timey.

JAMES. Crow! Crow! My God, it must be nearly twelve o'clock!

ROSIE. And poor Edmund searching in the forest all night. Oh, look! There's some villagers going off to help him. They all love him. Were you sity upy in sympathy with him? That's nicey. Cockadeedle-doo! There, you're free of your nicey gesture! My Jamie was such a clever, masterful Jame-Jame last night, arguing with Mund-Mund. And my Jame-Jame won.

JAMES (*absently, referring to cock*). What is the matter with him?

ROSIE. But Mund-Mund doesn't have to talkey: he looks it.

JAMES (*absently*). He looks it.

ROSIE. Such a lovely face. Such a sure face. I think he thinks you are his brother. Isn't he the sweet, kind silly billy?

JAMES (*angrily*). Crow!

ROSIE. Oh, I wish you were related. Then we would be nearer!

JAMES (*thinks he hears something*). Shh! – Shh! . . . (*Absently.*) Nearer?

ROSIE. Closer.

JAMES. Who?

ROSIE. Why, the three of us.

JAMES. For a start, pig, there's nothing between us.

ROSIE. You called me wifey yesterday.

JAMES. What does that mean, today or any day? Have we the bit of paper to prove it? Had we the rings, the candles, the bells, the balls, the first night, the honeymoon, the blushes?

ROSIE. Now, Jame-Jame, remember I wanted to –

JAMES. Jamie, Jame-Jame! My name is James! ROSIE!

ROSIE (*urgently*). Let's not quarrel, James, we don't want to quarrel, James, we vowed, we agreed a million times we wouldn't quarrel.

JAMES (*sneering*). And you believed? You believed?

ROSIE. Stop, James, please, I can't stand it!

JAMES. I can! I can!

ROSIE. You can't, James.

JAMES. Rosie! Rosie!

ROSIE. My name is –

JAMES. Rosie! Rosie!

ROSIE. Mary Ro –

JAMES. Rosie! Rosie! Rosie!

ROSIE. Mary! Mary! Mary!

JAMES. Rosie, the delicate thing, female!

ROSIE. Jame-Jame, sniveller, cry-in-bed dreamer!

JAMES. The middle-aged girl!

ROSIE. Thirty-seven!

JAMES. Hah! Get your supporting harnesses on, your teeth out of the cup, princess!

ROSIE. The princess that this corsetted ponce dragged into filth and scum, until she became filth and scum –

JAMES. You said it! – You said it! –

ROSIE. From *his* touch!

JAMES. You judge's get!

ROSIE. Behold: The prince!

JAMES. Slut, harlot!

ROSIE. The senile ponce! – How's your back?

JAMES. You excuse for a whore!

ROSIE. That kept you, dog, in bread!

JAMES. What about my kiss last night? – What about my kiss last night? –

ROSIE. Look at it! – Behold it! – Man! –

JAMES. Didn't it fool you? – Didn't it fool you? –

ROSIE. Look at it? Lover!

JAMES. Didn't it fool you for this morning?

ROSIE. Didn't I fool you by calling you strong and clever for last night? –

JAMES. Didn't I fool you? –

ROSIE. When I knew you were acting, pretending, loading the argument –

JAMES. I wasn't loading the –

ROSIE. Giving him the questions for your rehearsed answers?

JAMES. Not rehearsed! I wanted him to win!

ROSIE. Didn't I fool you? – Didn't I fool you?

JAMES. Oh, but I forgot, Mary Rose is in love with Mund-Mund!

ROSIE. Didn't I fool you when I knew you'd be chasing another rainbow today?

JAMES. But didn't I know you didn't mean it?

ROSIE. Look – look – look, out there, quick –

JAMES. Didn't I know you didn't mean it? –

ROSIE. Run and catch your rainbow, little crying cringing man!

JAMES. But didn't I know you didn't mean it, so it doesn't affect me! –

ROSIE. Didn't I know –

JAMES. 'Cause I had this quarrel planned! Now!

ROSIE. Didn't I know your twisted mind would be thinking that way? –

JAMES. And because I planned it, it hurts you more! Now!

ROSIE. And because I can see through your bottle-glass head spoils that! Now!

JAMES. But do you know the reason I didn't marry you all this time? Because now, when you look like pus and thirty-seven, I can laugh and walk away!

ROSIE. But who else would have you? Didn't you try-oi?

JAMES. And you didn't try-oi, I suppose?

ROSIE. Oh, but nothing can stop me loving Edmund and comparing him with you!

JAMES. But that's the poi-oint: nobody can stop you, *nobody* wants to!

ROSIE. But, really, you do compare very well with him, James, really.

JAMES. And you with Anastasia!

ROSIE. And, really, I shall go on loving him. It's simple, really, to love him: A man. Everyone loves him. Everyone loves you, Jame-Jame?

JAMES. . . . Rosie!

ROSIE. Everyone loves you, Jame-Jame?

JAMES. Rosie! – Rosie! – Rosie!

ROSIE. Mary Rose! – Mary! – Mary! – Prick!

JAMES. Whore, harridan, slut, shrew! –

ROSIE. Pencil prick!

JAMES. Oh yeah? – Oh yeah?

ROSIE. Unforgettable pencil prick!

JAMES. Oh yeah? – Oh – Shh!

Off, the cock crows. JAMES *delighted.* ROSIE *is suspicious but hides it.*

ROSIE. I mean, he's tall, good-looking, symmetrical, interesting, educated, elegant, speaks beautifully, assured, unwarty . . . Shall I go on? I've lots more.

JAMES *smiles, inviting her to continue.*

I pray he finds her, just to annoy you. Did you think I didn't know you would be after her? Mooching about in the wood yesterday. James and Anastasia! Tck! Pathetic! And your poor old back! It's too laughable.

JAMES. Finished?

ROSIE. That depends, thank you.

JAMES *trots most cockily into the cabin.* ROSIE *hurries after him.*

JAMES. Well . . . (*Gathers his thoughts.*) You don't know what I'm going to say to you now, do you?

ROSIE. Something inspiring. Maybe, 'You can't say two kind words to me'.

JAMES. No, my dear. Perhaps you should sit down . . . As you please. But this will come as something of a little shock. Well, I visited her last night. You know, *her*, hmm? While you lay gently sleeping. *I* have got her, *I* found her, she is hidden, safe and all mine. A short visit, necessarily, just to inform her that Edmund was dead. Tripped on a tree root, impaled on his sword. She insisted on – I mean, out of propriety, we agreed, mutually, yeh know, that there should be a short period of mourning; a period which might be spent profitably in considering the undesirability of force. And so, we agreed to be prepared for each other at cock-crow. As you can see I have kept my part of the bargain and, needless to say, she belongs to the equivalent honourable category in her sex. You're silent, my dear? But then you are thinking this is the pay off and you are right, so it is. But let us not be pecuniary in parting.

ROSIE. Acrimonious.

JAMES. . . . As you will, my dear, I meant exactly what I said, but as you will if it gives you solace. Rosie, you are through. But let us not be pecuniary or acrimonious in parting. I have grounds on which to be grateful to you, and I hereby acknowledge the amount of my debt. *You* were the ground on top of whom I made my first and last mistakes. (*He giggles, pleased with his wit.*) And yours was the oppression of some nineteen years' duration that encouraged my imagination to evolve principles on which I should conduct my life, given a second chance. Should you be interested I don't mind telling you that the course of those principles will see my young wife and I, pulling together, restoring the canary-bird of life to his former position, and confining the usurping cock to his proper place and time . . . Hmmm?

ROSIE. Am I expected to praise you?

JAMES. Well, perhaps you will show a more appreciative reaction to the unerring fashion in which I have developed matters when I tell you where my flower awaits me.

It strikes ROSIE *suddenly that* ANASTASIA *is hidden in the small room: her head swings about to look in that direction.* JAMES, *triumphant, trots to the door of the small room.*

Clever? Come now, you will admit the obviousness of the hiding place is its inspiration. Come, magnanimity! It passed the twenty-four hour test of your pocket-searching mind. No?

ROSIE. James, you're a loser.

JAMES. Think so?

ROSIE. I know so. I've lived too long with you, and you talk too much about success.

JAMES. Think so?

ROSIE. Edmund will be back.

JAMES. Too late! I am choosing to postpone, briefly, the introduction of the canary. So, should Edmund return, she will have taken the tragic step, voluntarily. He will be undone.

ROSIE. He won't, you know. He'll always be that comic step ahead of you.

JAMES (*laughs confidently*). Through your prayers, no doubt. (*Unlocking the door of small room.*) Pack your bag, my dear.

ROSIE (*losing her composure*). Close your eyes every time she spits!

JAMES. As you say, my dear.

ROSIE. You can't win!

JAMES. We'll see. Be gone when I come out. We shall see. And so, farewell.

JAMES *goes into the small room. His consternation on finding the vacant chair, looking incredulously at a piece of severed rope, a window which is firmly closed. He is searching on his hands and knees when* ANASTASIA *emerges from behind the door, gets the sword and has it held aloft to smite him when* ROSIE *gives the warning cry.*

ROSIE. James!

The cry gives halt to ANASTASIA's *stroke. She drops the sword, which* JAMES *catches, and runs out of the cabin.* JAMES *is transfixed with shock for a few moments. When he rises he moves about erratically, beating himself to allay his terror and frustration.*

ROSIE *is laughing – continues laughing to end of scene.*

ANASTASIA's *escape is confused and she circles the cabin a few times, her movement distracted.*

The lights are fading. JAMES *is coming out of the cabin to give chase, carrying the sword.*

Scene Seven

Another part of the forest.

ANASTASIA *is sitting on a height that overlooks a ravine, singing her suicide song.*

Through the song JAMES *enters stealthily (on the ground level below her).*

ANASTASIA.

I'm young but not too young to know
I've met the one I loved to love,
The one who wandered in my soul,
So tall and fine.
From early days my dreams did tell
His path and mine converging,

The cross-roads would be waiting,
As sure as sure can be.
And then he came and found me,
And I could have wept for mirth,
And the angels answered with a song:
Immaculate! Immaculate!
But now he's gone, no song is left,
Life is no more, I welcome death,
In yon ravine I go to join
My lost love so noble and fine.

She is about to throw herself into the ravine, JAMES *opens his mouth to call 'No' when*:

EDMUND (*off*). Anastasiaaaa!

EDMUND *sweeps in – or comes in swinging through the trees.* JAMES *in a frenzy of impotent gestures.* EDMUND *and* ANASTASIA *embrace, stand apart, embrace and apart again. Their two minds become one, excitedly gushing the following*:

But, Anastasia!

ANASTASIA. Oh, my Edmund!

EDMUND. Anastasia! –

ANASTASIA. Edmund! – Edmund!

EDMUND. But I knew I would find you!

ANASTASIA. I knew it too!

EDMUND. How lost was my feeling! –

ANASTASIA. But I would have died! –

EDMUND. Bursting the sky! –

ANASTASIA. Without you –

EDMUND. Anastasia –

ANASTASIA. Without you!

EDMUND. Then I heard your voice –

ANASTASIA. I did not know I sang –

EDMUND. From another world to guide me –

ANASTASIA. Cause our spirits were not lost –

EDMUND. But mingled in the ether –

ANASTASIA. Searching for the anchor –

EDMUND. Of each other –

ANASTASIA. And you came! –

EDMUND. We are found!

ANASTASIA. Forever! –

EDMUND. Together! –

ANASTASIA. Till death! –

EDMUND. And after! –

ANASTASIA. And even the past –

EDMUND. Was ours –

ANASTASIA. Yes! –

EDMUND. Yes-yes! –

ANASTASIA. All time –

EDMUND. Was made –

ANASTASIA. For sober –

EDMUND. Sublime –

ANASTASIA. Glorious –

EDMUND. Us! –

ANASTASIA. Us – us – weee! –

EDMUND   } The two of us!
ANASTASIA } The two of us!

They laugh.

JAMES, *a small figure below them, is now watching them in wonder.*

EDMUND. How much do I love you?

ANASTASIA. Mars, the stars! –

EDMUND. Nine hundred and eighty! –

ANASTASIA. Three million, ten million! –

EDMUND. Seventy-seven, billion trillion! –

ANASTASIA. Sufficiently –

EDMUND. Completely –

ANASTASIA. So much –

EDMUND. I am not me –

ANASTASIA. More than I can –

EDMUND. Because of you –

ANASTASIA. I am something great –

EDMUND. The trees in the streams –

ANASTASIA. I want to laugh or to cry –

EDMUND. Both are the same –

ANASTASIA. For being, for looking at you –

EDMUND. My lovely Anastasia –

ANASTASIA. Edmund, Oh my Edmund –

EDMUND. Will you be my wife?

ANASTASIA. Yes.

They kiss.

JAMES, *childlike, claps his hands once, silently, and stands for a moment wondering what to do. Then he hurries off excitedly.*

Scene Eight

Another part of the forest.

ROSIE *enters, carrying suitcase, as if leaving* JAMES. *But she is looking behind her, hoping* JAMES *is following her. No sign of* JAMES. *She sits on a log, sighs, smoking a cigarette.*

Then, JAMES' *voice, gallantly, off.*

JAMES (*off*). Rosieeeee!

   A moment later, JAMES *enters at a run, poses gallantly, sword held high.* ROSIE *exhaling smoke apathetically.*

ROSIE (*cynically*). Did you kill her?

JAMES. . . . Ah . . . No.

   ROSIE *turns away.* JAMES *trying to maintain his gallant effort against her apathy and, indeed, her appearance. His next call startles her a little.*

   Rosieeeee! I mean, Rosie . . . I'm very sorry, yeh know, about this morning. All our marital altercations. They shall never happen again. Forgive me, now, yeh know.

ROSIE. I'm used to it.

JAMES. Ah, the cigarette. Could you . . . ?

ROSIE. What?

JAMES. I mean —

ROSIE. Have you none, are you out, James?

JAMES. No — no, I'll have a puff.

   He takes the cigarette, has a drag of it to hide the fact that he merely wants to get rid of it. He stubs it out. ROSIE *is puzzled.*

ROSIE. I'm sorry too. What? And for laughing at you. Hmmm?

JAMES. Your hair.

ROSIE. It's awful.

JAMES. No, it's . . . not awful. (*He poses again, putting his foot on the log.*) Magic. Magic mirror on the wall, who is the fairest one of all? Rosie is!

ROSIE (*pleased*). Oh, James, what's wrong with you? (*Her hand stealing towards his crotch.*)

JAMES. No, no, but I mean to say, like, if you look at it this way, we waste an awful lot of time, Mary Rose, flower, and I could take you a million places. Three million!

ROSIE. But the money –

JAMES. No, don't mind that for now. Well, many places.

ROSIE } We could row.
JAMES } We could go to – What?

ROSIE. Row.

JAMES. Yes. We could row. We could . . . row.

ROSIE. Where to?

JAMES. Japan. To Europe.

ROSIE. Together?

JAMES. To the moon.

She laughs, pleased.

. . . We'll drink in life –

ROSIE. The Garden of Eden –

JAMES. Heaven –

ROSIE. And hell – just to see what it's like.

JAMES. And I'll protect you.

ROSIE. And love me –

JAMES. And love me –

ROSIE. And *me*, James –

JAMES. Yes!

ROSIE. Unceasing –

JAMES. Yes: That's it!

ROSIE. Till death us do part –

JAMES. And it never will, Rosie, Mary Rose, Mary!

ROSIE. Oh, Jimmy, we'll kiss our way to paradise –

JAMES. And the thrill of your kiss will constantly fire me to great things.

ROSIE. The thrill of a kiss!

They look at each other. They kiss nervously, shyly. Immediately there is a collapse.

(*Forcing a laugh.*) That was a laugh, James . . . We could try again. My fault. I didn't understand . . . Try again. I'll take one of my slimming pills.

JAMES. Don't bother.

ROSIE. What?

JAMES. They might help. (*He sighs.*)

ROSIE. They've got things in them.

JAMES (*harshly*). Naaw! Don't!

ROSIE (*tearfully*). Love you, James.

JAMES. Nonsense, bollocks, nonsense!

ROSIE. Love you, James.

JAMES. Oh, Jesus!

ROSIE. Little Jesus!

JAMES. Games, pretence! –

ROSIE. We could try again –

JAMES. I just want to stop!

ROSIE. We could try again –

JAMES. I was only trying for something, for anything.

ROSIE. For both of us.

Pause.

JAMES. I really do try, don't I? Tell me. I tried a lot of things, didn't I?

ROSIE. Yes.

JAMES. I mean, despite appearances, I've been on the go. So, it's not my fault, is it?

ROSIE. We don't understand.

JAMES. Who understands.

ROSIE. Nobody.

JAMES. . . . And don't let them tell you otherwise.

ROSIE. . . . Don't let them tell me what?

JAMES (*can't remember*). . . . That's more of it!

ROSIE. . . . We're two of a kind, James.

JAMES (*non-committal*). Mmm.

ROSIE. Birds of a feather . . . Flocked together.

JAMES. And the cow jumped over the moon.

> ROSIE *laughs*.

> And who'd blame him? . . . (*Then, sudden vehemence.*) I'll tell him a thing or two.

ROSIE. And her!

JAMES. Why shouldn't I?

ROSIE. Why not?

JAMES. I could mess him up.

ROSIE. Give him some facts.

JAMES. Then see his sunny world.

> *He takes up the sword and shows her the hilt.*

> Look at that! Just look at that!

ROSIE. A crest.

JAMES. The King's crest. That was a present from the King.

ROSIE (*produces* EDMUND's *water-flask*). And I nicked his water-flask. Oh look! It's (*the crest*) on this too.

JAMES. They'd fetch a pretty penny.

ROSIE. Stick to the point, James.

JAMES. Proper nancy-boy things.

ROSIE. No, give him some facts, James.

JAMES. When he comes back for those things –

ROSIE. Yes!

JAMES. I'll tell him about smells – worse –

ROSIE. Unmentionables! –

JAMES. Mention them!

ROSIE. The rotten teeth! –

JAMES. The nagging! –

ROSIE. Spectacles!

JAMES. What?

ROSIE. Other pathetic things!

JAMES. Pills! –

ROSIE. She wouldn't have them, he wouldn't! –

JAMES. Worse then!

ROSIE. People talking!

JAMES. Peeping-toms.

ROSIE. If they have one kid, why haven't they two.

JAMES. Or three –

ROSIE. Why haven't they four –

JAMES. Or six –

ROSIE. Why haven't they four –

JAMES. Or twelve –

ROSIE. Rabbits!

JAMES. Or none.

ROSIE. Or none.

They look at each other. They continue sadly.

JAMES. If we had a little girl, what would we tell her?

ROSIE. And she'd only turn out like me . . . And a boy . . .

JAMES. A son . . .

ROSIE. Like you.

JAMES. . . . Yes.

Pause.

ROSIE. Like scattered toys unable to play with each other, they
   say.

JAMES.

   God gave me a wonderful mammy,
   Her memory will never grow old,
   Her smile was fashioned of sunshine,
   Her heart was purer than gold.

ROSIE (*absently*). Once, in the dark, with a client, in that boxy
   room, in the silence, for a moment, a child cried from the
   heights of the floor above.

JAMES.

   It broke my heart to lose you,
   But you did not go alone,
   Part of Jimmy went with you
   The day you were taken home.

ROSIE. And from the depths of the floor below, from the
   basement, for a moment, the shuffling of that blind old man
   stopped.

JAMES. . . . Loving memory.

ROSIE. Scattered toys.

Pause.

JAMES. You know, Rose, if he ever knew – really knew – the way we are, the way we live.

ROSIE. Oh, if she knew, if she ever knew, James.

JAMES. Up on his high rocking-horse of morality . . . (*Vehemently.*) Think! What else can we tell them? But there are hundreds of horrible things! . . . Are you thinking?

ROSIE. I am, James.

JAMES. . . . But there are millions of rotten things!

ROSIE. Well . . .

JAMES. What?

ROSIE. Well, about men.

JAMES. What about men?

ROSIE. Well . . . how they're not so much men.

JAMES. Don't be afraid, don't be afraid, this is too important.

ROSIE. Masterful. I mean how he'll more likely be afraid of mice than she will.

JAMES. And how she'll more likely have to provide the bread!

ROSIE. And how men get tired of one bed!

JAMES. And women too – more often –

ROSIE. I agree, I agree. And how hard it is to find friends –

JAMES. That aren't enemies.

ROSIE. And not be their enemies for being friends.

JAMES. Yes – yes!

ROSIE. And about getting old!

JAMES. Yes! Get them with the obvious!

ROSIE. I'm doing alright, James, amn't I? –

JAMES. The surprise of the obvious.

ROSIE. But you do like me, James, don't you? –

JAMES. And success! 'Cause there's no such thing. – That's right – And how it looks bad, if they're nice or not nice to each other in public.

ROSIE. Yes. (*Apathetically.*) –

JAMES. And how they'll run out of conversation, hmm?

ROSIE. That's a good one –

JAMES. And . . . No, it would be no use.

ROSIE. How?

JAMES. You can never tell his kind anything.

Pause.

They continue, mellow.

ROSIE. But I must tell you, I'm pretty taken by him.

JAMES. Pretty taken . . . I was watching them in the wood.

ROSIE. I'm sure it was grand.

JAMES. Pretty taken . . . He's a prince, yeh know.

ROSIE. What? – Edmund? – A real one? – Really?

JAMES. Yeh.

ROSIE. Well-well!

JAMES. He's my brother.

ROSIE. What? . . . Aw, come off it! You're a prince too?

JAMES. No. No, I'm not. I'm not a prince. Yeh see, he's a half-brother, like.

ROSIE. Seriously?

JAMES. Serious.

ROSIE. But how?

JAMES. Well . . . a certain king who ruled at home come our ways one day to shelter in the barn out of the rain. And my mother, well, in the barn, they – she – well, Edmund's the King's son. The King even visited her before she died. Crest on sword, the (*water-flask*.) . . .

ROSIE. Well, I never! . . . So Edmund's a prince and you're not.

JAMES. That's about it.

ROSIE. That's not fair, James.

JAMES. That's life. (*He sighs.*) . . . Oh, I wasn't a peeping-tom at the time: it was natural, yeh know, for me to be in the barn. Well, I was a pious little lad and I'd decided for myself to work hard, around the stables and that, to help my parents out, so that if a baby brother came along, well, he would be given the chances, the money would be there for his education. Yeh know. Maybe I should have overlooked it, him being a king and all. But the tremors of that stormy day soon revealed other cracks in the walls, hitherto institutions with unblemished surfaces.

ROSIE (*suddenly*). Did he have his crown on?

JAMES. Aw, it's too depressing.

ROSIE. Poor love.

JAMES. I suppose you must know now, Rose, that I'm not at all well-educated. Sweeping out the stables. I've always lied about my education.

ROSIE. It doesn't matter.

JAMES. It does, it does. When I gam on (*pretend*) educated, I'm aping you.

ROSIE. We're very similar people, James.

JAMES. We are. And a confession: I'm always thinking I'm better. But we are. Even a few minutes ago when you said, we're two of a kind –

ROSIE. Birds of a feather –

JAMES. I didn't want to agree. Yeh know?

ROSIE. I understand, James.

JAMES. But we are.

ROSIE. We have an awful lot in common.

Short pause.

JAMES. Do you remember, Rose – Wait a minute. Were we? . . . Yes! When we were in love. Do you?

ROSIE. . . . We wouldn't –

JAMES ⎤ We wouldn't go to bed at night!
ROSIE ⎦ We wouldn't go to bed at night!

JAMES. Trying to stay awake!

ROSIE. In case we'd miss a single second of it all.

JAMES. I wanted to be you.

ROSIE. I wanted to be you!

JAMES. I wanted to be you!

ROSIE. You wrote me poems, James.

JAMES. I thought – Don't laugh – I used to imagine if only the two of us could breathe from the same lungs.

ROSIE. Beautiful . . . What happened to it?

JAMES (*gesturing as if pricking a balloon with a pin*). Puck! Sssssssss!

Pause.

ROSIE. I thought we might stop all this kind of thing here . . . And you were planning to leave me.

JAMES. How do you know that?

ROSIE. Instinct. A woman's. And you often thought of it before . . . What do you think?

JAMES. What?

ROSIE. About leaving me.

JAMES. Did you ever think about leaving me?

ROSIE. I did, but I wouldn't.

JAMES. You're nicer than me, Rosie. Really.

ROSIE. I am not, James, I know it.

JAMES. No. I know better. I'm rotten. And I'm afraid of what I'm going to be like in ten years' time.

Pause.

ROSIE. We aren't succeeding with anything here.

JAMES. Hmm? . . . I don't know.

ROSIE (*absently*). Hmm?

JAMES. I don't know, Rose. 'God gave me a wonderful mammy': I said that easily enough.

ROSIE. Hmm?

JAMES. I shed that easily enough.

ROSIE. Hmm? . . . (*Like a first realisation.*) But we're very good friends, James.

JAMES (*absently*). What?

ROSIE. We're very good friends.

JAMES. What? . . . (*Coming alive.*) What? What? Aren't we? We are! What? . . . And do you know it's as good as – it's better than – What? – it's much better than love!

ROSIE. Yes, but we can still love, now and again.

JAMES (*not listening*). Yes, we can, but we're very good friends, Rosie. We are very good friends.

The excitement of the feeling makes him trot about.

ROSIE. Where are you going?

JAMES. What? . . . No, I wasn't going anywhere. Have to move.

He stops, looks at her.

I enjoyed that little chat.

They smile at each other, then look away shyly.
They look at each other again and start to laugh, enjoying the warmth of the moment.
They laugh so long it tends towards hysteria.

ROSIE. Dear, oh dear! . . .

JAMES. Maybe we'll be crying in a minute . . .

ROSIE. What harm. I feel so good.

JAMES. Oh, don't trust it, Rosie!

ROSIE. . . . Taunting us again . . .

JAMES. . . . I just got an idea! . . .

ROSIE. Let's not scheme, James . . .

JAMES. Oh, it would keep us laughing for a while . . . If we were in bad humour we'd use it.

The laughter grows weaker, sporadic. JAMES *stops;* ROSIE *stops a little later.*

ROSIE. What were we laughing at?

JAMES. . . . That's more of it!

ROSIE. I felt so grateful. (*A titter escapes.*)

JAMES. Why should he have it all when the world treats us this way?

ROSIE. So indiscriminately.

JAMES (*sharply*). I know – I know! Why don't I just go along and acknowledge him as my brother?

ROSIE. That's because – (*Another titter escapes.*) because you're ashamed of yourself.

JAMES. Oh! Is it? You understand it all, do you, with your guilt-ridden little Jesus education!

Pause.

ROSIE *smiles evilly a moment before* JAMES *speaks.*

If they were like us . . .

ROSIE *nods, continues smiling.*

What?

ROSIE. Yesss.

JAMES. If we can't get to their ridiculous level, they must be brought to ours. What?

ROSIE. I'm way ahead of you. I've most of the spade-work done.

JAMES (*he grins appreciatively*). A taste for gin.

ROSIE. And he has kissed my hand, my cheek . . .

JAMES. . . . When he comes back for those things – (*The sword, the flask.*)

ROSIE. A pleasure, James. Round three coming up.

JAMES. And, meanwhile, I'll look after the orphan. Let's get a few details worked out.

They hurry off.

Scene Nine

Night. The cabin. The cabin appears transformed. (Softly lit; an arrangement of flowers; soft music.) ROSIE *and* EDMUND *are eating.* ROSIE *wears a nice or sexy dress.* EDMUND *appears quite drunk.*

Outside, JAMES *is hovering impatiently in the background, eavesdropping, waiting to hear where* EDMUND *has left* ANASTASIA.

ROSIE. You're too sensitive, they used to say to me, Edmund. I thought it very shrewd of you to spot that at a glance. But I was an only child, you see. 'There must be other fish in the sea, mother' daddy would say to mummy, 'as an insurance against this one': Me. But wasn't it a jestful, meek and mild way of putting it from such a harassed man? Wasn't it? More gin?

EDMUND (*laughs*). 'Tis nice stuff.

ROSIE (*filling* EDMUND's *glass*). Isn't it? And there were seven in all in my home town, once upon a time, wanted to marry me. Marriage, oh yes, no lie, Edmund, seven. As honest as their ungroping hands. They liked me for myself, you see. But I was looking for one and lost myself. Forever. Hmmm?

EDMUND (*laughs*). 'Tis nice stuff.

ROSIE (*defensively*). I mean, I don't know why I'm remembering these matters now, because they're just — statistics — to me. I don't get involved, not anymore.

EDMUND (*laughs*). A feast.

ROSIE. Once I knew two complete recipe books by heart. (EDMUND *laughs*.) My hometown. And daddy would rap the kitchen table with his little toy gavel that mummy gave him for Christmas, and he would say 'Order, Order, mother, girl! *I* will now say Grace.' And he would. Such pure security you cannot imagine. (*She takes up the gin bottle, brushing*

away a tear. She finds the gin bottle empty.) I loved daddy.
He reminded me of God, and Uncle Joe.

EDMUND (*laughs*). 'Twas a feast.

ROSIE. Well, not bad for one little gas ring. Let me get some
more gin.

ROSIE *goes into the small room for another bottle of gin.*

JAMES *races around the cabin and speaks to her angrily
through the window of the small room.*

JAMES. What's all the sham-talk for? Get the poxy score and
ascertain where he's left the orphan?

EDMUND (*calls*). But 'tis pity James could not be here!

ROSIE. 'Tis a pity, 'tis. But he must be a hundred and fifty
miles away by now. (*Returning to* EDMUND.) And he won't
be back 'til morning.

JAMES *trots to front of house to eavesdrop the better.*
ROSIE *fills glasses.*

EDMUND. Sad. A good fellow is James. I had wanted to bid
him farewell.

ROSIE. We were wondering if you found your brother.

EDMUND. Now that, Mary Rose, is strange. My body is not
satisfied —

ROSIE. Yes, Edmund?

EDMUND. Yet spirit says my quest is done.

ROSIE. How strange!

EDMUND. My body is not satisfied, yet spirit says, my quest is
done. Is it not 'ceeding strange?

ROSIE. How very strange! And the villain?

EDMUND. The villain, ah, the bane! I started here in search of
. . . ah . . . ah . . .

ROSIE. Three.

EDMUND. Three. I have found one.

ROSIE. Yes, I wanted to ask you, how is dear Anastasia? Where
have you left her?

EDMUND. Found one. Found one.

ROSIE. Where have you left her, Edmund?

EDMUND. How kind you are to enquire and let me speak of
the little one I found! How you would love her!

ROSIE. But where have you left her?

EDMUND. Aaa, if only she were here! But such is the rule of
wedding's eve, that we one night must separate, and wear
divorced affiancedment in vidual weeds, to give point to
spouselessness!

ROSIE. Oh, and to give pause, Edmund, to heady rush towards
imminent connubiality!

EDMUND. Aa, quaint conservative pain, sweet I salute your
mandate celibate! But to reflect my course – to pause? – I say
go bid Niagara halt!

ROSIE. Fine, okay, but where have you left her?

EDMUND. But she is left in honest hands, in the house of
friendly rustics, westward on the hill.

   JAMES *races off.*

ROSIE. That's all we – I wanted to know. That she is safe.

EDMUND. Safe? Yes! For as I strode away, from foot of slope I
lookéd back to see my trusty friends in human chain, well-
police that hut. All armed with heavy bludgeons held aloft
were they, no heathen phallic signs they meant, but to assure
this humble groom, the chaste strength of Anastasia's belt!

ROSIE *hurries to the window to warn* JAMES, *but* JAMES *is gone, and she can only shrug. Then she has perhaps a premonition about the outcome of her own course, but she shrugs this off too and turns up the music.*

And yet, aa, if only she were here!

ROSIE. Yes, well, we're glad she's safe, but that's all I want to hear about her. And now you must listen to the music.

She leads him to the bed. They sit.

EDMUND. How kind you are to enquire and allow me speak of my loved one!

ROSIE ⎱ Yes, but the music –
EDMUND ⎰ (*moves away from bed*). And from afar I lookéd back again to see the sun had chose this night, that very hill where my love lies, to rest its rubic head!

ROSIE. But listen to me now, Mary Rose –

EDMUND. And, Mary Rose, tomorrow's geography will place her home upon the spot, within a vale, wherein the sun doth rise.

ROSIE. The sun follows her – smell them flowers.

EDMUND. The sun follows her, I swear!

ROSIE (*gives him the flowers*). What fragrance! I say! A token to you, Edmund.

EDMUND. I have known a flower to shed more sweet a –

ROSIE. But you'll agree they smell nice? You'll agree to that for a start.

EDMUND. But yes! A toast in scent!

ROSIE. A toast in scent!

EDMUND. To think that eager nature should be first in her well-wishes for the morrow!

ROSIE. The music, Edmund! – That's for tonight.

EDMUND. Sweet, unreal, of fairies.

ROSIE (*drops the stole off her shoulders*). Soft.

EDMUND. Only once before have I heard softer. A song in the forest, so pure it was a pain –

ROSIE. More wine, Edmund, the mead. (*She fills his glass several times during the following.*)

EDMUND (*accepts*). 'Tis nice stuff. Easing my anxious vigil for the morn that will bring my first dawn; a solace to this alone spirit that endeavours to push on the night to those first modest blushing streaks, the keys to my unity with dawn herself!

ROSIE. Oh, Edmund.

EDMUND. And yet, that is not all true. Yes, you are right, Mary Rose. This gin that quickens my tongue, has not so much solaced my yearnings as enhanced them. Making me almost want these clouded hours to delay in sweetest – sweetest taunting-hauntingness!

ROSIE. Then let us lie on the bed, your hand in mine.

EDMUND (*not listening*). And with sense acute to slothful moments now –

ROSIE ⎱ Edmund –
EDMUND ⎰ Know that the hours – Nay, the years, the
                centuries! – following my morning union will be
                the more appreciate!

ROSIE (*taking his hand*). Edmund –

EDMUND (*leads her to the window*). Come! You will watch the heavens with me! Look! See the clouds sweeping a path for the feet of dawn! I have found her! (*Shouts.*) I have found her! Have I told you? Today, Rosie!

ROSIE (*alarmed, confused*). Mary Rose, Mary!

EDMUND. Down in the forest there was no crow, Rosie –

ROSIE. Mary Rose, Mary!

EDMUND. And my body fed, even to the skin, with a fullness as I looked at her!

ROSIE (*laughing harshly*). Brains danced on like grapes to make abortions!

EDMUND. And once I closed my eyes to trap the angel self within me, but no feature was left me! All of me had fused to become one sensitive eye! And it went on: drinking in God, or was I radiating Him, or was I Him?

ROSIE (*laughing harshly*). I say my head is sore!

EDMUND. And you too, Mary Rose, must have felt all this.

ROSIE. Rosie, Rosie, my ageing fancy grows more incapable!

EDMUND. What can I give to you, splendid earth, for all you are giving me!

ROSIE. Come to my working blanket, kiddo!

EDMUND (*approaching her*). And in what way can I thank you?

ROSIE. I'm still alive, kid!

EDMUND. Your garb is so thin.

ROSIE. The fire of your presence is warmth for any maiden! See? Not bad? Think of the here and now. (*Dancing.*) See: Am I not alive? – See, simple alive.

EDMUND. You are all that, and more.

ROSIE. Then just a few of your gifts, baby!

He dances with her for a moment, then stops.

Just a dance! Just a dance!

EDMUND. Understand you must that fidelity's single breach –

ROSIE. All is a song, nothing is wrong for a hero, baby, they say!

He laughs, he starts to dance.

EDMUND. The flowers increase their presents.

ROSIE. Inhale them, inhale!

EDMUND. The violins are careering towards crescendo!

ROSIE. Climb with them to the heights for the cascade, baby!

EDMUND. Anastasia – Anastasia!

ROSIE ⎱ (*harshly, to drown him*). Come, follow, for the
⎰ crusade, baby! (*She climbs on to the bed carrying the gin bottle.*)
EDMUND ⎱ Anastasia, Anastasia! (*dances to the elevated level of small room.*)

ROSIE (*sinking on to bed*). Exhale from every pore the sweat for our cohesion! Fuse the ache, confuse the pain into joy! Lips around your heart, strengthen me with passion! Come, follow, hide in my wounds, bleeding together, font of love, impaled on life, struggling, pulsating, driving, bolting, throbbing, spurting, scorching, crushing, holy, cannon, war! Crusade-cascade-cascade-cascade! Edmund – James, Jesus – Daddy, Little Jesus – Oh my baby – Us all together! (*Joyfully.*) Everyone is fucking great, every one is smashing! . . . Everyone . . . sinking . . . Cascade! (*She giggles.*) . . . slowly, down . . . into the feather meadow . . . (*Sleepily.*) Peaceful, peaceful, and wait so peaceful, us all together, soon again, the ferris wheel, toboggan and cascade. Hush, drowse, Mary Rose. Little Jesus, meek and mild, thank you for life and sleep.

EDMUND. Rosie!

Short pause. ROSIE *sits up, suddenly.*

ROSIE (*whispers*). Don't.

EDMUND. Whore!

ROSIE (*whispers*). Don't!

EDMUND. Why this betrayal?

ROSIE. I thought I had a plan –

EDMUND. Wherefore this attempt to sap my foundations? –

ROSIE. I thought I had a purpose –

EDMUND. From whence this evil? –

ROSIE. But my heart is shrivelling, tightening, getting small, something has to happen or it will tighten into nothing!

EDMUND. Your heart is in your belly.

ROSIE. Forgive me!

EDMUND. Never!

ROSIE. Once I was a nightly abstainer, a morning communicant!

EDMUND. Wretch!

ROSIE. Daddy was a Judge, Uncle Joe a Bishop!

EDMUND. Jade!

ROSIE. Seven in all in my home town wanted to marry me!

EDMUND. Fetor! (*He is strapping on his sword and water-flask, preparing to go.*)

ROSIE. No – Don't go! – I'll tell you things. James and I are not married – I've been on the game, in and out of the club. Don't go. I'll tell you things. James is your brother.

EDMUND. Stop, vileness! And I suspect that this serpent man of yours had a fang in this night's doings. I have a mind to wait and let the venom from his veins, but I will bear this devil's pad no more; but will await my dawn alone, out in the dew where I'm afforded a view without stench, and with nothing to fear but the sweetness of nature.

He goes out of the cabin. The first streak of dawn appears in the sky. He exits smiling.

After a few moments JAMES enters, limping, looking beaten-up, goes into the cabin and sits.

ROSIE is sitting on the bed, a painted-up whore. Both of them silent, dejected.

Scene Ten

The part of the forest, as in Scene One.

JAMES enters using a walking-stick, limping. ROSIE carrying her suitcase, a moment later. He taps the ground with his stick, indicating that they will wait here.

ROSIE. Maybe they've gone off already.

JAMES. No. They will have been getting married. Jingle bells, yeh know, and those dirty hayseed natives giving ignorant cheers.

ROSIE. They might have.

JAMES. Gone away? And left us here so happily on our own? . . . Gone off where?

ROSIE. I don't know.

JAMES. Then what are you talking about?

ROSIE (*malice; watching him limping*). . . . And are your ribs still sore?

JAMES. Are you sure you didn't know what I was letting myself in for last night?

ROSIE. No, I swear, James. Honest.

JAMES. . . . And when you said I was his brother, he said?

ROSIE. 'Stop, vileness.'

JAMES (*muttering*). Stop, vileness.

ROSIE. I misjudged him. And I felt I had him on the point of it!

JAMES. When you said I was his brother, he said?

ROSIE. I didn't want to tell him, James, but —

JAMES. He said! — He said!

ROSIE. 'Stop, vileness.'

JAMES. Well, that's alright then, isn't it? 'Stop vileness.' That's fair enough, isn't it? That's what we wanted, isn't it? Well, I shall have only one final word to say to him, one little wedding gift.

We see that the walking stick is a sword stick.

Yeh know. Now.

ROSIE does not look too happy.

What?

ROSIE. But what if *you* get killed, James?

JAMES. So what? (*Then unconvincingly.*) So bloody what, Madam? No confidence in me, never had, always held me back. Colleagues could do it. I was meant to be a ruthlessly practical idealist.

ROSIE. It's a big step.

JAMES. You won't even encourage me to try? . . . 'Stop, vileness' and you're not offended? You said today you had a feeling it was him who was trying to seduce you last night. Not offended? In the middle of his golden days and sunny islands and kisses sweeter than wine, he balks, you're confused, off your guard and he's in with a Judas-punch: Not enough to kill, oh no, just to damage. Not offended? . . . You agreed with me at the start that I should wait here and have it out.

ROSIE. I know I did, but . . .

JAMES. What?

ROSIE. It's a big step.

JAMES. I know it's a big step! . . . What?

ROSIE (*quietly*). And what then?

JAMES. . . . . We'll see! (*Angry.*) Well, give me an honest-to-God
butchering murderer to deal with then. He'll do his job
smartly. He won't ask you to kill yourself, will he? chasing a
picture that isn't there, while he smiles on his approval, until,
in the end, you stop, drop dead, no heart left, death-rattling,
lights out, no picture! What? You prefer it this way! . . . I'm
doing this for you too. I'm thinking of you too, Rose. I've
been from pillar to post, pub to pub; I've abused you, Rose,
and neglected you; I've been thro' thrice nine lands chasing
cloud number seven, sixteen, a hundred and two, any old
cloud they cared to lie on, and I've come back to you a bigger
bastard every time, with the pox and my guilt! Are – you –
not – offended?

ROSIE (*quietly*). And her.

JAMES. What?

ROSIE. You're right, James.

JAMES. Of course I'm right.

ROSIE. Kill them. The two of them. But be especially cruel to
her. Let them see each other age with pain, before you give
the dying kick, (*Harshly.*) baby. Make them writhe, toss,
implore for an end, like when sleep won't come a second
night. Baby. I want to see her eyes afraid to move in snuff-dry
sockets, and know that acid streams of jealousies are slowly
burning channels through her head. Give them the pains of
the lack of pains of motherhood. The pain of the secret
birthmark, unwanted hair, wanted hair. The pain of the small
bust longing for the big bust and the big bust longing for one
a little bit smaller. The sanctity pain of puritan plain-Janes.
And all the skin pains, from black to anaemic, until their
pores are gaping holes. The pain of revenge. And the breath
of fresh air, once, somewhere, and the pain that follows it
because of it, breathing the stale, coffin-smelling, stifling,
suffocating air of the mind. Nothing achieved but memories –

that pain. Not being able – Don't let them be able – kill them, kill them, kill them.

JAMES. I will, Rosie, I will.

ROSIE. Are you sure?

JAMES. Of course I'm sure. We have all that evil and the devil behind us.

ROSIE. No devil, no evil, no God, no crap.

JAMES. What?

ROSIE. We've tried all that. Kill them in our own name.

JAMES. That's what I've been saying! I like it, I like it!

ROSIE. Let it be a fact.

JAMES. Let it be a fact, a basis.

ROSIE. Then we'll see.

JAMES. First, I'll have him begging relationship off me, then I'll –

ROSIE. Save it, James. Let us not dissipate our intention. Rather, let us fortify ourselves with a festering silence.

JAMES. . . . Shh!

EDMUND *and* ANASTASIA *enter, a beautiful couple, coming through the trees.*

ROSIE. Say something to them. Shout at them.

JAMES (*running to intercept them*). Stop, vileness! Stop, vileness! Stop!

ANASTASIA. Oh, the villain, Edmund, the bane!

EDMUND. Fairest of all, I commend my heart to you for the brief space of a minute.

JAMES (*in fighting pose*). I'm ready, I'm ready.

ANASTASIA. Oh adult Edmund bold, a favour –

JAMES. No favours –

ANASTASIA. Do not dampen this our wedding day with blood.

EDMUND. Granted.

JAMES. No, I'm ready now!

ANASTASIA. Smile on them instead, and may happen some good will come of it.

EDMUND. For in death they will rot and give out only worse stench.

ROSIE. Start insulting them.

JAMES (*to* ROSIE). Dignity.

ANASTASIA. James, though a villain, has a point left.

ROSIE. May your smugness turn black, your virginity become as barren as a barrel, your —

JAMES. Dignity, bitch! I must stay cool for this one.

EDMUND. And Rosie, though unmentionably employed, may not be the worst in the world.

JAMES. She is the worst in the world and I'm the worst in the world!

ANASTASIA. We have forgiven you both.

ROSIE. Don't let them forgive us.

EDMUND. My young wife's pleasure.

   EDMUND *and* ANASTASIA *moving away.*

ROSIE. Don't let them get away.

JAMES (*running, intercepting them*). Stop, vileness! If I remember correct, you started here in search of your brother.

ROSIE. In search of three, James.

JAMES. Quiet, madam, don't spoil my flow!

ANASTASIA. He has found me.

EDMUND. I have found the villain.

JAMES. But being noble, like, you can forget your original purpose over this young scrubber.

ROSIE. Good, James.

JAMES. She is a tartlet.

ROSIE. She would have prostrated herself for the first long-haired prick that came along wearing feathers.

JAMES. Her puppy-fat type abounds.

EDMUND (*hand on sword*). The lowlies, true to form, in bravery assail the character of the bride.

ANASTASIA. Forbear, husband, we shall find you a nice brother on the way home.

JAMES. You have found your *nice* brother.

EDMUND. Do not detract from my tree.

JAMES (*to* ROSIE). Quick, what does that mean?

EDMUND. I said do not detract from my family tree!

JAMES. Mine too.

EDMUND. I give you warning!

JAMES (*to* ROSIE). He won't admit it.

ROSIE. 'My body is not satisfied, yet spirit says, my quest is done.' Strange, is it not?

EDMUND. Mark their ugliness.

JAMES. Your brother's ugliness.

ANASTASIA. How much lovelier we look by comparison.

JAMES (*giggling*). Aa, he's getting rattled.

ROSIE. Keep your head, James.

JAMES *and* EDMUND *circling each other.*

EDMUND. You are taking advantage of my bloodless pledge.

JAMES. I couldn't care less about your pledge.

EDMUND. You are one to be denied.

ROSIE. He denied you first.

EDMUND. Prove your claim, prove it!

JAMES. It's a fact, it needs no proof.

EDMUND. Oh, the strange fact is that one who has agreed to unrelation all along is now so eager for connection.

JAMES (*to himself*). Quick: what does that mean? (*To* EDMUND.) I'm not eager to be anything to you.

ROSIE. On the contrary.

JAMES. On the contrary, I'm not eager to be anything to you.

EDMUND. Then wherefore bring the subject up?

JAMES (*growing confused*). Then wherefore bring the . . . I-am-your-brother! You-are-going-to-admit-that. Then-I'm-going-to-have-done-with-you and deal-with-you-absolutely!

EDMUND. Ridiculous.

JAMES (*confused*). What? (*His statement dismissed so easily.*)

ANASTASIA. Ridiculous.

JAMES. Be quiet, you orphan! I can give you proof!

ROSIE. He can give you proof.

JAMES. I can give you –

ROSIE. Names, addresses –

JAMES. Who's who and what's what –

ROSIE. Apple trees –

JAMES. And meadows, now, yeh know!

EDMUND. All this news I told to you myself.

ANASTASIA. The night they pulled you down to ginny pub-crawl.

JAMES. There was a kind old midwife . . . what was her name . . .

EDMUND. Yes, what was her name?

JAMES. . . . There was a lame but kindly sweet-shop man . . .

EDMUND (*to* ANASTASIA). Our town is famous for non-limping men.

JAMES. Before your time! – Before you were born!

ROSIE. Get on to the spotty details of your genealogy.

JAMES. And Teddy Bear had lost an eye and not his ear!

EDMUND. Oh no!

JAMES. Oh yes! Teddy Bear had lost an eye and lived up in the attic.

EDMUND. Aha! (*Got you.*)

JAMES. What?

EDMUND. Under the stairs.

JAMES. What?

EDMUND. Teddy Bear lived under the stairs! (*To* ANASTASIA.) I mentioned the attic to trap him.

JAMES (*to himself*). In the closet under the stairs, in the closet under the stairs.

EDMUND. And father's name was softer one than Stones.

JAMES. Jones!

EDMUND. Or Jones.

JAMES. I know! – I know!

ROSIE. Your mother, James, before he tells us.

EDMUND. I have told you all about my mother.

JAMES. And *my* mother too. My dear old sweet mummy. God gave me a wonderful mammy, her memory will never – (*Savagely.*) No, naaw, no! I've settled that score.

EDMUND. And that is that! The imposter has exposed himself. I must confess I was unsure, but my final doubt he has dispelled just now. My brother James, though beautiful, could not at all speak well of ma: This flaw he had – 'twas not his fault, and so she said. A mental aberration caused by horse's kick when being forced to unclean stall.

ROSIE. Tell him about the randy king before he tells us.

JAMES (*quietly*). No.

EDMUND. The mental aberration, aforesaid, did manifest its lunacy by latching on to accident my mother had. For she did once, attending a tea-party of the King, a tiny slip when curtsying.

ROSIE (*incredulous*). The lies!

EDMUND. 'Twas but a moment's totter from the combinated cause of hem and over-zeal, confronted by the awesome right divine. As you can see, and so she said, 'twas but a trifling faux-pas, but enough to make a mole-hill from the late, lamented, mountain brain of James.

ROSIE. Too late.

JAMES (*quietly*). No.

EDMUND. And so, farewell.

ANASTASIA. Our memories will visit you.

EDMUND (*leading* ANASTASIA *away*). To the sun!

   JAMES *withdraws sword from stick.*

JAMES. Thou monstrous faux-pas!

EDMUND. What's this?

JAMES. You're going nowhere any more. The crow has come for you. Defend yourself if you like; it's all the same to me.

EDMUND. It cannot be helped.

ANASTASIA. Then be not too severe.

They come together to cross swords.

EDMUND. And another thing I know, my brother James was no swordsman.

JAMES. Prepare yourself for a fencing lesson, and for death.

*They sword-fight. EDMUND looks expert. JAMES'
knowledge of swordplay comes from films about pirates, but
even this degree of finesse soon deserts him. The fight grows
abandoned and bizarre, JAMES racing about, going through
a series of mishaps, pathetic, ridiculous, his desperation
increasing until, eventually, he starts to roar in frustration
and charges at EDMUND, both hands flailing, wielding
sword-stick and its wooden scabbard. EDMUND is thrown
by JAMES' total abandon and he loses his sword. The point
of JAMES' blade is at EDMUND's neck. JAMES hesitates.
EDMUND is smiling confidently.*

ROSIE. Kill him!

*This sort of victory is not good enough for JAMES. He drops
his sword, pretending he is unable to kill EDMUND. Then he
walks away, his hand covering his eyes, as if he were crying.
A glance backward to see if EDMUND is following him.
EDMUND comes to JAMES, embraces him.*

EDMUND. Now I know who you are.

*Still embracing, JAMES withdraws his knife from under his
coat, and as he stabs EDMUND in the back –*

JAMES. Now you can be sure of it.

*EDMUND, dying, falls behind the trees. JAMES starts to sob.
ANASTASIA hurries to help EDMUND. ROSIE takes
EDMUND's sword, follows, and kills ANASTASIA. ROSIE
joins JAMES. Both crying through the following.*

ROSIE. We done it, James.

JAMES. We did.

ROSIE. . . . What have we done?

JAMES. . . . We'll see.

ROSIE. . . . It's nice to cry, James.

JAMES. . . . Don't be fooled by it, Rosie.

ROSIE. . . . You can't trust it, James.

JAMES. . . . We might be laughing in a minute.

They exit crying.

The Sanctuary Lamp

Characters

HARRY
MONSIGNOR
MAUDIE
FRANCISCO

A church in a city.

Introductory and bridging music from 'The Sleeping Beauty'
(Tchaikovsky)

To Noel and Mary, Murt and Dorothy,
Vincent and Patsy, Fergal and Brid,
Andy and ?

ACT ONE

Scene One

A church. Late afternoon light filtering through a stained-glass window – the window depicting the Holy Family; great columns to dwarf the human form; a pulpit; a statue of Jesus; a confessional tucked away somewhere; and a lamp, the sanctuary lamp, in a container suspended from the ceiling. (Other features as required, as benefits director's/designer's ideas. The sacristy and vestry mentioned later are assumed to be off.)

HARRY is seated hunched in a pew. He is in his forties; unshaven; we recognise him as a down-and-out; his rumpled suit/overcoat, though the worse for wear, gives some indication of his childish vanity and reflect former better years. And an affectation in his sound ('y'know?' 'old boy' etc. – British officer type) but it started a long time ago and is now part of his personality.

An elderly priest, a MONSIGNOR, is pacing slowly up and down reading a book. A touch of cynicism (his recurring invitatory short laugh: 'What?'), disillusioned, but a very humane man.

And MAUDIE, whom we see later, is fifteen/sixteen; a waif-like thing about her.

HARRY is now considering MONSIGNOR; he coughs, raises his hand tentatively, to get Monsignor's attention. MONSIGNOR looks enquiringly at him.

HARRY. Y'know!

MONSIGNOR. Hmm?

HARRY. Excuse, but, Padre – is it? Padre? Padre? – Is there anything you can suggest?

MONSIGNOR. Hmm?

HARRY. Quite frankly I'm intelligent, I'm a very strong man, and you may think it a paradox but I do not know how to get out of the puzzle I am in.

MONSIGNOR. Yes?

HARRY. Excuse my butting in 'cause I can see you are – y'know? But something on my mind, dire need of help and I'm not talking about soup.

MONSIGNOR (*considering* HARRY). Hum, hum, haa! There's just a chance that . . . What's y'r name?

HARRY. Harry, sir – Padre – Henry.

MONSIGNOR. Harry?

HARRY. Stone.

MONSIGNOR. I see. And what've y'been doing with yourself then, Harry?

HARRY. Well, actually, it's not quite that.

MONSIGNOR. Hmm?

HARRY. Well, casual work, actually – if you must know. And very occasional casual work recently. And begging, frankly.

MONSIGNOR. I see.

HARRY. But it's not quite a question of that. This compulsion to do this – terrible thing. Y'know?

MONSIGNOR. Yes?

HARRY. But I didn't do it.

MONSIGNOR. Good.

HARRY. No.

MONSIGNOR. Yes?

HARRY. The compulsion is there to go and do it now. And a feeling of wrong-doing because I haven't gone back to do it. A terrible deed! So what am I to do?

MONSIGNOR. Yes?

HARRY (*surprised/confused by* MONSIGNOR's *seeming blandness*). What? . . . To get the question straight for myself! But, demoralisation – y'know? Deterioration – y'know? And worse, more confused by it all by the day.

MONSIGNOR. What business were you in, Harry?

HARRY. What?

MONSIGNOR. What has led to your – present circumstances?

HARRY. The financial side?

MONSIGNOR. If you like.

HARRY. Well, though not very important as I said, they never stamped my cards – y'see? – and that's difficult to explain at the Labour Exchange.

MONSIGNOR. I see. And who are 'they'?

HARRY. In the circus. I was the strong man.

MONSIGNOR. Were you indeed? Fancy that!

HARRY. Oh yes. But when there was a general cutting-down on things, when it became unviable – y'know? Unviable? – to feed the larger animals, they asked me to muck in with this act. Me, Francisco, Olga, and the dwarf. Contortionist, Olga, actually. Getting herself into distress. It wasn't circus.

MONSIGNOR. So you left?

HARRY (*hedging*). Well, I . . . Hmm?

MONSIGNOR. So you packed it in?

HARRY. Ah – Hmm?

MONSIGNOR. Hum, hum, haa!

HARRY. Would you like me to tell the truth? (*A single slow nod of the head from* MONSIGNOR.) Well, when we'd have done our act we were obliged to wait around for the grand finale. Quite a bit of time to kill, actually, because we did not top the bill. And I did not think it was proper for Francisco and Olga to spend that time alone. So we spent it all together. And Francisco – not Italian, not Spanish, a juggler, actually – has this interest in religion – holy religion? Mind you, so do I. The Gentiles? Holy Gentiles? Anyways, quite a bit of time to kill, all together, all quite correct, until one night the subject of holy religion comes up and . . . (*He hesitates.*)

MONSIGNOR. A row broke out. (*He chuckles.*)

HARRY. Well, just three blows, bum – bum – bum, one for each of them.

MONSIGNOR. And you got the sack?

HARRY (*chuckles with* MONSIGNOR). Indeed. Indeed.

MONSIGNOR. Yes?

HARRY. Oh, but we still stayed together.

MONSIGNOR. Yes?

HARRY. Went – y'know? – freelance? Quite adventurous, mind you, some of the engagements we got but . . .

MONSIGNOR. Yes?

HARRY. Not very ennobling.

MONSIGNOR. I see. Anything else?

HARRY. Ahm, this . . . (*He still wants to talk about his 'compulsion'. He changes his mind.*) No. You were going to say, Padre?

MONSIGNOR. Well, as it happens, our clerk died three weeks ago last Wednesday. The bishop sends around one of his young priests occasionally to help out. With a guitar. But no replacement for old Bill. Otherwise I should not be here at two o'clock in the day reading Hermann Hesse, what? I should be at home by my fireside reading Hermann Hesse. D'ja read, Harry?

HARRY. Oh yes.

MONSIGNOR. Lovely stuff. I don't know how I've missed out on him for so long. But as to the job of clerk here, it's yours as far as I'm concerned, if you're interested.

HARRY. Job?

MONSIGNOR (*he is searching his pocket and producing an envelope which he uses as a bookmarker*). Actually causes me physical pain to turn down the corner of a page. Ridiculous, what? (HARRY *shifts a little. He has not expected this offer.*) You're not sure?

HARRY. Not quite that – y'know? – but . . . Clerk?

MONSIGNOR. Oh! Silly sort of name for it, really. No, the sort of thing that if someone comes along and wants a Mass said, you write in the diary Mass for N on such-and-such a day, Baptismal Cert for so-and-so. I'd hardly call it clerking. Soon get used to it, soon get bored by it.

HARRY. Padre.

MONSIGNOR. Your duties, mainly, would be to do with . . . (*He pauses to watch* MAUDIE *who has entered to cross the background, glance shiftily at them and exit.*) To do with keeping an eye on the place. Locking up at night before you go home, and opening up again in the morning. Okay?

HARRY. Padre.

MONSIGNOR. Pay's not much, I'm afraid – Are you married?

HARRY. No.

MONSIGNOR. Hmm?

HARRY. Y'know?

MONSIGNOR. Thirty-nine pounds a week. Let me show you around. Ridiculous, I suppose, in this day and age, but, there you are. This is the Vestry. Sort of my domain. And over here is the Sacristy. Soutane is supplied, second-hand but dry-cleaned and that, and who knows but it may have been the bishop's. What? D'ja know him? The bishop?

HARRY. No.

MONSIGNOR. And this is the Sacristy, sort of your domain, your kitchen so to speak. D'ja know him to see?

HARRY. Indeed.

MONSIGNOR. Yes. Little gas-ring in there for your elevenses. That sort of thing. Please ask any questions. And that confessional over there: old Bill, your predecessor – if you decide to take the job – old Bill used it for the brooms and things. Yes?

HARRY. W.C. in there?

MONSIGNOR. Yes. And you have your hand-basin over there. (HARRY *nods thoughtfully*.) . . . Hmm?

HARRY. Nightwatchman?

MONSIGNOR. No. You would have to see that everything is securely locked up before leaving each night.

HARRY (*reflectively*). Very handy.

MONSIGNOR. Okay?

HARRY. Padre.

MONSIGNOR. Oh, by the way, I'm a Monsignor. Silly sort of title really, but, there you are. Okay?

HARRY. Okay.

MONSIGNOR. And this of course is the sanctuary lamp.

HARRY. First thing I noticed.

MONSIGNOR. Signifying the constant presence.

HARRY. It's a mystery I suppose.

MONSIGNOR. I suppose it is. Despite all the modern innovation this still needs personal attention, so you would be required to replace the candle every twenty-four hours.

HARRY. It shouldn't go out. (*Eyes fixed on lamp.*) First thing I noticed. (MONSIGNOR *looks at him.*) And the silence. I'll accept the position.

MONSIGNOR. You're clear on what has to be done?

HARRY. Leave it to me.

MONSIGNOR. Splendid. Well, let me take your address. Formality for the bishop's office. (*Poised to write in his diary.*) Yes?

HARRY. Certainly.

MONSIGNOR. Yes?

HARRY. 22 Paxton Street.

MONSIGNOR (*writing*). Paxton Street. Very good. (*He glances at his book as if eager to be away.*)

HARRY. Though, mind you, I won't be very often in.

MONSIGNOR. No. Very good. Any other? (*Questions.*)

HARRY. Do I – ? (*He mimes pulling a bellrope.*)

MONSIGNOR. No. That one's alright. Electronics, what?

HARRY. Monsignor.

MONSIGNOR. Splendid. (*Both are pleased with themselves. MONSIGNOR is looking around to see what next to show to HARRY.*) I do wish the wages were a bit better, but – Well, let's see how you get on. Let's see now. Yes. (*He is about to lead HARRY off when he gets a sudden thought.*) Oh, by the way, you are a Catholic, aren't you? (*They are looking at each other: mutual dismay beginning to appear. HARRY*

gives a single nod, hopefully, in the affirmative.) . . . What's
the most dangerous animal in the circus?

HARRY. The horse, actually.

MONSIGNOR *gives a slow single nod. Then, leading*
HARRY *off, as the lights change and bridging music comes*
up.

MONSIGNOR. The switches for the lights are down here . . .

And MAUDIE *is entering, to stand there looking after them,*
as the lights fade.

Scene Two

Night. HARRY, *now dressed in a soutane, is climbing or*
standing in the pulpit to inspect the pendant sanctuary lamp the
better: the old candle does not yet need to be replaced. He sighs.
The church clock starts to chime ten. He begins to feel the
church and the night closing in on him.

HARRY. What is it, my soul, already?

He comes down from the pulpit, pauses to consider the
trunk-like base of the pulpit . . . Next, he faces the empty
church, flexes his muscles and calls:

All out!

Then into action, exiting and entering with a large bunch of
keys, locking doors. Then he extinguishes the lights and the
sanctuary lamp comes more dramatically into relief. In the
unaccustomed dark he bumps into something and growls; he
bumps into something else and emits a growl of rage as he
pulls off his soutane and squares up to the pulpit. To the
lamp:

See! See!

He tries to lift the pulpit and fails. To the lamp:

Why do you resent me? . . . And being watched here as no
servant – as no menial! – was ever watched before. I have
every right to be here! (*Then to himself, selecting a key from
his large key-ring.*) Every right. I thought he'd be back to lock
up with me. But then he may show up yet. So – (*He pockets
the selected key.*) Y'see? That's okay. (*His purpose beginning
to falter, dismally.*) I'd be as well off in the park again tonight
. . . (*Addressing the lamp again.*) I won't be staying here for
nothing! . . . You get nothing for nothing, that's business,
isn't it? Well, then. So I'll bung a deuce of quids into (St.)
Anthony's box every Friday . . . y'know? . . . And we're all
God's children, whatever religion . . . (*He begins to feel he
may have misinterpreted the lamp.*) Of course it's not a
question of the money with you either. Or – (*He imitates the
whispering sound he has heard people make when praying.*)
What? Like calling a cat! (*He moves slowly, circling the lamp,
then sits looking at it.*) The silence turns to loneliness, Jesus?
Time passing . . . My spirit is unwell too. They've been trying
to crush my life. They even had me wrestling with a dwarf –
with Sam, y'know? – and he had to win. I don't mind being a
clown but I'm not a fool. So, supposing we can come to some
arrangement, I have every confidence I can get well here.
Supposing in exchange for the accommodation I engage to
make good conversation – break the back of night for you?
(*To himself.*) Alleviate the holy loneliness. (*To the lamp.*) But
there would have to be a time limit. Supposing I say till two
a.m.? Till three? What's a fair time? Till three is generous,
and by my reckoning that will be about the time to replace
the candle. I wish he'd told me the proper time to do it. So
that's settled then. What shall we talk about? . . . Not a very
busy one today, Jesus? No. Not a very busy one. No . . . You
know Francisco? Juggler actually. Well, he was my friend, I
took him in. Then he usurped, sneaked my wife. And now he
lives – my greatest friend! – quite openly with her. And we
had brought a child into the world . . . I wouldn't have let a
thing like that go by a few years ago. (*He looks at the pulpit.*)
And I'd have waltzed around the room with that. (*He
retrieves his soutane.*) Do you think madness must at least be

warm? I don't mind telling you I keep it as a standby in case all else fails. (*He suspends the action of putting on the soutane.*) You never feel your soul when you're happy. (*He starts to dance; movements vaguely balletic and reminiscent of a child's. Then:*) And sometimes, in the mornings actually, she'd toddle up to my bunk, toddle up to my bunk, bright little eyes – very bright, mind you – arms tightly round my – (*neck*), and laughing, laughing, admiring her daddy – y'know? y'know? – admiring her daddy. Teresa. (*A noise off. He listens. Silence. He continues to button his soutane.*) I was very famous too. And always careful of my dress. (*He sits.*) The Duke of Windsor, he was a well-dressed man. Knew him – David, y'know? – first names, David, very charming. (*The clock chimes the half hour. He rises as if having somewhere to go. Impotence, nowhere to go and he sits again.*) Only half-ten . . . Oh, but I have every confidence of our little arrangement proving mutually fruitful, so let me think again . . . (*Then growing agitated, he rises suddenly.*) But-if-I-stop-to-think-I-only-start-to-think of my daughter-daughter-daughter, Teresa! No one to feed the wonder in the eyes of a child. Help me to forget! You who rule the heavens and the earth, stretch forth your mighty arms therefore: help me to forget. (*He sits.*) And once out walking, and a shower of rain, and no other shelter, so naturally I put her under my jersey. Like a little bird nestling – I could even feel her heart – and she even fell asleep there. Frankly proud of that. But then I'd think of the years ahead and people like myself already laying traps, and then I'd look into her eyes and I'd feel I must cry, or my breastbone must certainly snap in two. (*Another creak off. He listens. Then he forgets it.*) You know Olga? Wife actually, Olga. Well she was very lonely. And she seemed – y'know? Superior? – ladylike type of person. Told me she'd been a ballerina once. (*She*) May have been daydreaming, of course. And I was one of the best sports, so we became married. And we had Teresa. Then she started to say, look at you, you disgust me, just look at you. And, when I tried to swap the lonely thoughts of the small hours with her, that I bored her actually. Olga. Real name was Winifred of course.

And then Francisco sneaked her. Then she started to say,
'People!' – Like that – 'People!' . . . Then, me in the bunk,
Teresa in the cot, eyes open to the night, through the night,
every night. As if no one else in all the world. Time passing.
As if no one else in all . . . space. In silhouette – that's it,
that's it, in silhouette. Little girl and a man, standing black on
the edge of the world, the edge of it all, looking out at all the
sad, slow-moving mists of time and space. And me such a
strong man and could do nothing. (*Suddenly.*) Where do you
go when you die? . . . I made some attempt to alleviate of
course, and after lights-out pretended to teach her some
tables. Up to seven times. Just in case she understood. And
little lectures on history. Italy – y'know? I was there. But
there are limits to tables and lectures on history, and
eventually I'd say 'night-night' – y'know? – 'night-night' –
and wait. Then just the occasional – (*He mimics the double-
beated cough of a child.*) Just the occasional – (*He repeats the
cough.*) to punctuate, time passing . . . Of course all this time
Olga was off, having herself screwed, panting for unhappy
life in the very next room. With Francisco. Or making love to
all and sundry. Nothing could flower . . . Then always there
would come a point: time passing would stop – and this
terrible thing come knocking at my heart. *Keeps* knocking at
my heart. But I kept on hesitating. Night after night this
thought would come: well, if as they say there is no law, there
is no God, mustn't I take charge? . . . Once I did get up,
penknife opened, pounding heart, I thought I'll do it now.
Nothing on my daughter's face to urge me to kill them. Still, I
thought, I'll do it now. Then looked into their room. Nothing
but a burning light of hatred – Invitation! – from the
darkness from their eyes. Then I'd say if I was mad I'd do it.
If I was mad I'd hurry back and do it now. But I do not want
to be like them, I believe in life! And I kept on hesitating till
all I could do was lie there with the child. Because no one
should be on their own. It's even bad for a dog . . . And then
of course she died. But very interesting – I was very surprised
– all I could do was say what does it matter, and left. Well, I
waited till we got our next engagement – quite an important

engagement actually, I wonder how it went? And to punish them, I walked away. Well, sloped, actually, to let them down. (*He pauses: the awareness of the inadequacy of his retaliation makes him stand suddenly in frustration. He starts to lurch at the pulpit.*) I sloped away! (*He checks himself. Then, intensely:*) Oh, Lord of Death, I cannot forget! Oh Lord of Death, don't let me forget! Oh Lord of Death, stretch forth your mighty arms, therefore! Stir, move, rouse yourself to strengthen me and I'll punish them properly this time! (*A noise off that sounds like a sob. He listens. Silence.*) Every confidence. (*He listens again. Silence.*) Still, I wonder how that last engagement went. Isn't that surprising? (*A creak off. He listens. Another creak. HARRY is motionless. He thinks it is FRANCISCO. He takes out a penknife and opens it. Whispers:*) Ah, very shrewd Francisco, very cunning. (*To lamp:*) Thank you. (*Loudly:*) Ah – excuse for just a moment. (*He exits.*)

MAUDIE *is entering cautiously. A light is switched on revealing her fully, her tear-stained face, her fear, and* HARRY *is entering with his penknife. The sight of her stops him.*

HARRY. What are you doing here, Miss? – Don't scream! . . . What is the meaning of – y'know?

MAUDIE. You frightened me.

HARRY. What?

MAUDIE. You frightened me.

HARRY. Did you come here to burgle?

MAUDIE. I was here first.

HARRY. What? You don't work here! This pad goes with the job. Yes it does! (*She runs: he intercepts her.*) How long has this carry-on been going on? (*She starts to cry.*) Tears to no avail! . . . Shh! . . . Haven't you nowhere else to go? . . . Shh! . . . There, there now . . . There, there now . . . y'know? . . . Are you hungry? . . . Don't move. (*Gets his jacket from*

*which he produces two slices of fruit cake wrapped in paper.
He offers her a slice of the bread.*) Would you like a slice of?
. . . Stoller. Fruit cake . . . Time was when stoller was the
only sweetmeat I allowed myself. (*Offering bread again.*)
Hmm? . . . And I was a great believer in liver, raw eggs,
brown bread and yogurt . . . Hmm?

MAUDIE (*accepts*). Ta.

HARRY. Y'see? I thought you might be hungry. I always kept
myself well. What's your name?

MAUDIE. Maudie.

HARRY. What?

MAUDIE. Maudie.

HARRY. That's a very nice – y'know? Very charming . . . Why
are you dossing here, Maudie? (MAUDIE *is unforthcoming.*)
And I was always proud of my lightness of step. Many people
commented on it . . . Alright?

MAUDIE. Cold.

HARRY (*looks at his jacket*). Actually, this has got a slight
odour about it.

MAUDIE. There are cloaks in there.

HARRY. Hang about. (HARRY *exits to the vestry and returns
with a vestment which he puts on her.*) Y'see? . . . Hmm?

MAUDIE. Who else is here?

HARRY. No need to be frightened. The Presence.

MAUDIE. Jesus?

HARRY. Not quite. It's his spirit actually. They nabbed his
spirit and they've got it here. It's a mystery of course but
that's what religion is. (*She looks at him.*) Personally, I think
they should let him go but, there you are.

MAUDIE (*indicating statue*). That's Jesus, isn't it?

HARRY. That's Jesus . . . Do you adore him?

MAUDIE (*looks at him*). Do you?

HARRY. No. Y'know?

MAUDIE. Neither do I.

HARRY. I've great respect for him, mind you.

MAUDIE. He gives forgiveness.

HARRY. A very high regard. A veritable giant of a man, if you want my opinion, but between one thing and another, his sense is gone a little dim. And who would blame him? Locked up here at night, reclining – y'know? – reflecting his former glory. So a bit of diversion helps.

MAUDIE. But he gives forgiveness.

HARRY (*sharply/defensively*). How do you know? He doesn't have to forgive me. I did nothing wrong. I don't reproach myself. So, y'see? You have to commit the sin first to get that. But, properly approached, of course, he can still do other things. Would you care to? (*Sit.*)

MAUDIE. And he likes children, doesn't he?

HARRY (*looks at her for a moment*). Well, of course he does. The holy booklets down there: *Suffer the little children to come to me.*

MAUDIE. Ay?

HARRY. Hmm?

MAUDIE. Suffering?

HARRY. No. Suffer. Suffer, in our parlance means, please allow. Please allow the little ones to come to me, that's what he used to say.

MAUDIE. . . . Are you a priest?

HARRY. Not quite.

MAUDIE (*first smile – a shy innocent smile – from MAUDIE*). I didn't think you were.

HARRY. I'm the clerk. Assistant monsignor, y'know? Silly sort of title really, but there you are.

MAUDIE. Who's that then?

HARRY. Joseph, y'know? Mary's spouse, Joseph. I've always had a soft spot for Joseph. I've always felt he must have been a bit lonely. Though, mind you, there's some that say she had other children. Quite a large family of them in it, I've heard a person say, so, maybe one of them had a bit of time for him. Joseph.

MAUDIE. No, who's the little boy.

HARRY. Oh! That's the Infant.

MAUDIE. He's my favourite.

HARRY. Not mine. I'm quite fond of children, actually, but he's too clever-looking by half for me.

MAUDIE. I like him best.

HARRY. What does your mam and dad think about your staying out at night like this? . . . Do they punish you? Do they beat you? (MAUDIE *shakes her head.*) What?

MAUDIE. Grandad.

HARRY. Do you stay with your grandad? (*She nods.*) Hmm?

MAUDIE. And gran.

HARRY. And do they punish you? (*She nods.*) For staying out? (*She looks at him.*) Is that why you don't go home? (*It's not the reason: she doesn't want to talk. She averts her eyes.*) . . . I haven't much time for her either. Mary. It was a good idea alright: holy family — y'know? — the three of them. But see that expression of hers? I know someone like that. And she was a Catholic too. But of course it was all a front to conceal a very highly-strung neurotic nymphomaniac. Where's your dad, Maudie? (MAUDIE *gives the slightest shrug.*) Where's your mam? (MAUDIE *is unforthcoming*.) Are you still hungry? (*She nods*.)

MAUDIE. And tired.

HARRY. But, we don't want to turn in yet. It's only – (*Eleven o'clock*.) A bit of diversion – conversation – And made a promise to replace the – Here, I only need a little piece of this. The smallest piece of food in the stomach prevents an ulcer. (*He gives her the major portion of the other slice of bread*.)

MAUDIE. Ta.

HARRY. Y'see?

MAUDIE. Are you going to send me home?

HARRY (*disappointed*). When?

MAUDIE. Tomorrow.

HARRY. But I didn't think you'd want to.

MAUDIE. I don't want to.

HARRY. Well then. (*She smiles*.) But we'll have to be careful. (*She agrees. Both are pleased. A few surreptitious glances at* HARRY *and* MAUDIE *decides to talk*.)

MAUDIE. Do you know John Wayne?

HARRY. Indeed.

MAUDIE. . . . Not personally.

HARRY. Ah . . . No. No, I know quite a few of that – elite, y'know? – but not John Wayne.

MAUDIE. Well, he is one of grandad's favourite heroes.

HARRY. Oh yes?

MAUDIE (*nods*). Well, one night he weren't much use, and grandad come home, sad, with gran, from the ABC.

HARRY. They were unfulfilled.

MAUDIE. Sad.

HARRY. Oh yes?

MAUDIE. And I were standing at our gate and didn't see in time. And grandad gave me a hiding. Because I'd put my foot outside the door. And then he put his boot to the telly. Because it were snowing. And the telly-man said it were no accident, and grandad had to pay. And grandad said he'd have no telly in the house again, even if it were to choke him.

HARRY. Black and white?

MAUDIE. . . . What?

HARRY. The telly.

MAUDIE. Yes.

HARRY. But why weren't you meant to put your foot outside the door?

MAUDIE. . . . What?

HARRY. You're – y'know? – big girl . . . Where's your mam?

MAUDIE. *My* mam? (*He nods.*) *My* mam is dead.

HARRY. Oh . . . When did she . . . ?

MAUDIE. When did she die? (*She smiles.*) I think it were a few years ago.

HARRY. Oh yes?

MAUDIE. Well, do you know 'dreaming'?

HARRY. Oh yes?

MAUDIE. Do you?

HARRY. Indeed.

MAUDIE. Well, I don't know. I never saw my mam. Not that I
remember. I saw my dad alright, but I never saw my mam.
They went their separate ways, gran said. Well, (a) few years
ago, I started to – dream – about my mam. Then I knew she
were dead. But I think she were really visiting me. But gran
said, dreaming. But I don't agree. But gran said 'dreaming,
Maudie, dreaming' and not to be dementing her and not let
grandad hear. (*She looks at* HARRY *for his appraisal.*)

HARRY. Oh yes?

MAUDIE. Well, grandad heard and said I were a whore's melt.
And gran said then I were a millstone. (*She smiles at*
HARRY.)

Note: *To* MAUDIE, *this story is essentially one of personal
triumph.*

HARRY. Oh yes?

MAUDIE. Well, do you know 'in bed'?

HARRY. At night?

MAUDIE. Yes. Her face would come beside me, in the dark,
like a plate. And her eyes would look at me. And I didn't
know what to say. So then I'd look about for gran. Or even
grandad. To say something. But when I'd look around again,
my mam were always gone. And then I'd try to scream. To
fill the room again. But I couldn't scream. And it went on like
that. Like, every night. Like, forever. (HARRY *nods.*) Well,
one night, I knew there were a change. She were not staring
at me any more. She were looking down. More peaceful. Like
reading the paper. Or thinking it out. And I looked about to
see if gran had seen this change for the better. Gran had seen
alright, but she wouldn't pretend. And I knew that when I'd
look around again my mam would still be there. And she
were. And I waited. But then my mam got up – (MAUDIE
gives a haughty toss of her hair.) My mam got up and went
out. I were so disappointed. I think I were going to cry. But

then the door opened again and my mam were standing there, and she looked at no one else, and she said, 'Oh, by the way, Maudie, I'm very happy now.' And I were so grateful. And then I told my gran, whether it were dreaming or not, it were all over.

HARRY. And what did your gran say?

MAUDIE. She said it were forgiveness. (MAUDIE *smiles her personal triumph and* HARRY *complements.*)

HARRY (*to sanctuary lamp*). That was very successful. That was very – y'know? But why do they punish you now?

MAUDIE. . . . What?

HARRY. Y'know?

MAUDIE. . . . Do you know 'lamp-posts'?

HARRY. In the street?

MAUDIE. Yes.

HARRY. Oh yes?

MAUDIE. Well, there's one outside our house, and I've been able to climb it since I was eight.

HARRY. Ropes attached?

MAUDIE. No.

HARRY. Shinning?

MAUDIE. Just my hands and knees. And because gran and grandad would be out, at every change of programme since the telly broke, I'd go out and climb the lamp-post. And the other children would pull back to watch. (HARRY *chuckles, identifying with the experience.*) Sometimes I'd climb even higher than the light. I would catch the iron thing on top and pull myself up over the top, and sit there in the night. And sometimes, if I waited up there long enough, everything made — sense.

HARRY (*a little jealous of this last experience*). Did you ever hear of Ivan the Terrible?

MAUDIE (*nods, but she is not listening to him*). It were very exciting.

HARRY. That was my name when I topped the bill.

MAUDIE (*nods*). And then I'd come sliding down and the others cheering, 'Maudie — Maudie — Maudie!' That's what they always said. 'Maudie — Maudie — Maudie!' Except — it were funny — when two of the older boys that sometimes come along, and they always said 'Maud, Maud!'

HARRY. Pass that ball of paper — Maud. (*They laugh. She hands him the paper that wrapped the bread.*)

MAUDIE. 'Who taught you how to climb poles, Maud?' And I'd say 'Jesus!' (*They laugh.*) And sometimes I'd come sliding down and then I'd do cartwheels. Do you know cartwheels?

HARRY. Oh, indeed.

MAUDIE. Or stand on my head? (*He nods.*) Or there were another. I'd come sliding down, I wouldn't have stopped, but keep on running into our house, and I'd open the window, and I'd have stood on the table, and I'd've took off my clothes, and stick my bottom out at them. And they'd be cheering 'Maudie — Maudie — Maudie!' And the two bigger boys —

HARRY. Maud! Maud!

MAUDIE. Yes. 'Maud, Maud, come out a minute'. Sort of whispering.

HARRY. And would you? . . . go out again?

MAUDIE *is now looking gravely at him. She nods. Now she is near tears.*

MAUDIE. Shall I tell you?

HARRY. No –

MAUDIE. Shall I not tell you?

HARRY. No, that was quite successful –

MAUDIE (*crying*). But it's started up again –

HARRY. Another topic – what shall we talk about?

MAUDIE. Not dreaming – not dreaming! –

HARRY (*trying to think of something to offer her*). I know: would you like – would you like –

MAUDIE. I just want it to stop –

HARRY. Maudie, would you like –

MAUDIE. Forgiveness. Forgiveness.

HARRY. Maudie, Maudie.

MAUDIE (*dismally*). Shall I not tell you?

HARRY. Old favourite actually. (*Sings.*) 'When the red red robin goes bob-bob-bobbin' along. When the red red robin goes bob-bob-bobbin' along. Get up, giddy up' – Maudie.

MAUDIE. What?

HARRY (*indicates a pillar, jocosely inviting her to climb it*). Would you?

MAUDIE (*then laughing, drying her tears*). It's too fat.

HARRY. Do you know any songs? Hmm? And then I might go out and buy some – Well, let's see how we get on. Do you know any songs?

MAUDIE (*sings*). 'Put your head upon my pillow; hold your warm and tender body close to mine; hear the whistle of the raindrops blowing up against my window; and make believe you love me one more time; for the good times, for the good times, for the good times.'

HARRY. That was very nice. Hmm?

MAUDIE. Tired.

HARRY. Yes. It's important that you get your sleep. Where do you sleep?

MAUDIE. In one of those boxes. (*The confessionals.*)

HARRY. In the vertical? Too ventilated in the vertical, and bad for the circulation. We can be getting it ready. (*He starts to remove the brooms etc. from the confessional.*) The horizontal gives better protection against the breezes. So, we'll lay it on the floor. I think we're safe now against the Monsignor showing up.

MAUDIE. And there are plenty of cushions and things about.

HARRY. Yes, start collecting a few of them. (*She goes.*) But remember where you took them from! We can get in a little store of tea, sugar, brown bread and butter tomorrow. And jam. Actually, the most thing we need – it crossed my mind today – a little extractor fan for in there. (*The sacristy.*) With a little extractor fan no odours of cooking about in the morning. Would you like a drink of water? (*She nods.*) Follow me.

She follows him to the threshold of sacristy and stands there. He exits for a cup of water. She considers the sanctuary lamp for a moment.

MAUDIE. Is he (*Jesus*) awake?

HARRY (*off*). Oh yes. (*Returning.*) And starting tomorrow we'll buy some utensils. (*He gives her the water.*) We'll buy a pan – if the Monsignor thinks to sub me. And when we get our pan, we'll cook some nice calf's liver, and onions. And if he doesn't think to give me the subbies, we'll have to tap St. Anthony – (*He chuckles.*) for the short term. Enough?

MAUDIE. Ta. (*She hands him the cup. HARRY exits with the cup.*) Does he sit on a throne?

HARRY (*off*). Do you see a throne? (*Returning.*) Well then. No, more like a wheelchair, if he's sitting on anything, but we'll soon take care of that. And a little bit of decoration around here would do no harm. (*The clock starts to chime twelve.*) Yes, I think we're safe now. (*He catches the top of the confessional. He pauses for a moment.*) If we could think of the proper place to put the fan.

MAUDIE. We could stay here forever!

HARRY (*lowering the confessional to a horizontal position on the floor*). Hup! Hup! Voilà! (*They laugh at their confessional-bed. They are delighted with themselves. HARRY – the circus strongman – skips back from the confessional.*) Ivan the Terrible! Voilà! Voilà! (*He considers the pulpit momentarily: rejects idea. He strikes poses.*) Here, Maudie! What am I doing? Holding back six horses! Here, Maudie! You be my assistant. Like this: watch! (*He demonstrates the movements he wishes her to perform. She obliges.*) Then say 'Voilà!' 'Voilà!' Means, 'See!' 'Behold', actually, that's what it means. (*He is lying on his back on the floor.*) What am I doing? A plank across my arms and chest, lifting four, six, eight, ten tall men!

MAUDIE. Voilà!

HARRY. Hup! (*He is on his feet again: considering the pulpit.*)

MAUDIE. You nearly lifted it. I was watching.

He is going to the pulpit, then changes his mind, smiles to himslf. Now his movements balletic, reminiscent of a child dancing.

HARRY. No. Everything is alright now. I'll look after you, Maudie.

MAUDIE (*reacting to something off*). Shh!

HARRY (*to himself*). It was no simple stroke of luck that led me here.

They are reacting to a noise outside. He takes out his knife.

Francisco? (*Listens again.*) The governor's here! Hurry, quick, cave!

He sends her off down the church, he grabs an armful of the cushions – there isn't time to stand and replace the confessional – and hurries off in another direction. During this the MONSIGNOR is heard unlocking the sacristy door. MONSIGNOR enters. He stands looking at the comparative disarray, the confessional lying on the floor, etc.

MONSIGNOR. Harry? . . . Harry! . . . Anybody here?

FRANCISCO has entered the church, secretly following MONSIGNOR. We see him briefly – perhaps only as a shadow. He hides. MONSIGNOR begins to move in the direction that MAUDIE has taken. HARRY enters.

HARRY. Ah – Monsignor – Excuse! But I waited on to do a few chores . . . That old confessional: I thought I'd give it a good scrub out tomorrow. If walls could talk!

MONSIGNOR. Yes. I'm sorry. I had meant to be back to lock up with you but I got caught up in . . . (*The book.*)

HARRY. Actually, I thought you might, so – y'know? (HARRY *picks up the paper that wrapped the bread, holds it out so that* MONSIGNOR *can see it is a thing of nothing and puts it in his pocket.*)

MONSIGNOR. So . . . I think everything is in order.

HARRY. Excuse for just a . . .

HARRY *lifts the confessional, returning it to its proper position.* MONSIGNOR *watches him and sighs, now understanding the better* HARRY's *state and circumstances.*

MONSIGNOR. Thank you, Harry.

HARRY. Monsignor.

MONSIGNOR. So, I think everything is in order. (*He is reluctant to leave: wandering what can he do for* HARRY.) Yes, I got caught up in the book. Finished it.

HARRY. Good?

MONSIGNOR. Yes. Yes, it was, actually. (*The awareness of the futility of his day's achievement in his smile.*) So . . . (*He makes a move as if to leave.*)

HARRY. Ah – Excuse – But – (*He indicates the replacement candle which* MONSIGNOR *has picked up.*)

MONSIGNOR. Oh. That's alright. (*He leaves the candle somewhere.* HARRY *momentarily concerned for the lamp.*) Were you happy in the circus, Harry?

HARRY. Oh yes. Well, early on. Before I – y'know? Actually, in my category, I was rated one of the four strongest men in the world.

MONSIGNOR. Were you?

HARRY. Y'know?

MONSIGNOR. Yes.

HARRY. Sixteen stone weight above my head before I was sixteen.

MONSIGNOR. Yes, I saw you were a cut above the average.

HARRY. But I don't mind admitting I'm very happy here.

MONSIGNOR. Yes.

Pause.

MONSIGNOR } Is there anything I can –
HARRY   } Is the –

MONSIGNOR. Yes?

HARRY. Is the Pope infallible?

MONSIGNOR. Well, the last one was, the next one will be, but we're not so sure about the present fella. Anything I can do for you, Harry? . . . Things go wrong for people, don't they? All of us need help one way or another . . . In my own case, I'm not sure what went wrong. Was led to expect a certain position some years ago, and when the seat – position – became vacant, I was passed over in a regular piece of church jiggery-pokery, and fobbed off with one of the new semi-detacheds – detacheds – that were built with the new school. What? . . . No, of course I had no right to allow myself to be led to expect anything, had I? No, the real reason: lost my humility. If I ever had any. Humility, what? A cunning way of dealing with God. Yes. Well, point is . . . what is the point? (*He laughs to himself.*) That wasn't much help, was it? What I'm saying is, I'm not a totally lost soul and I've never turned anybody away from that same semi-detached. Detached. Extraordinary word. (*To enunciate.*) I can offer people shelter. What do you say?

HARRY. I've a very good head for heights actually, and I know where you can hire extremely excellent scaffolding – mobile kind, on castors, y'know? and I wouldn't mind having a go at painting that ceiling.

MONSIGNOR. Hum, hum, haa!

HARRY. Only cost you the price of the paint.

MONSIGNOR } No, what I'm saying is –
HARRY   } No charge for the labour of course.

MONSIGNOR. People stay at my place from time to time –

HARRY. Goes without saying, labour would be gratis –

MONSIGNOR. Until they get fixed up. Plenty of books there, that sort of thing.

HARRY. But do you not see the roof is falling in! (*Then by way of apology for his sharpness he adds.*) Y'know?

MONSIGNOR. Yes. Shall we? (*Go*) (*He is going to switch off the lights: stops.*) But, just for your information, Harry, before coming here I called to the Paxton Street address to see if you'd managed okay. Chap there, cheeky chappie, had some drink taken I think: Said you didn't live there anymore. I thought I'd tell you: he seemed — eager — to find you. I didn't tell him where you were.

HARRY (*muted*). Monsignor.

MONSIGNOR. You're more than welcome to stay at my place until you get things straightened out.

HARRY (*firmly, to himself*). I'm going to get things straightened out. May I – y'know? (*Go*)

MONSIGNOR (*searching his pockets for money*). I'm afraid I came out without any –

HARRY. Tut-tut, of no account. Seven-thirty in the morning then?

·MONSIGNOR. Why don't you call and see me at ten, or eleven. Whatever time suits you best.

HARRY. Monsignor.

And exits purposefully. MONSIGNOR *switches off the lights and exits a moment later.* MAUDIE *appears cautiously: she stands there looking after them.* FRANCISCO *appearing from behind a pillar.* MAUDIE *retreating to the shadows,* FRANCISCO *following her: he stops, whispers.*

FRANCISCO. Excuse me! . . . Excuse me!

Music up, lights down.

ACT TWO

Scene One

Half an hour later. MAUDIE and FRANCISCO in the church. FRANCISCO is drinking a bottle of altar wine. He is in his thirties; Irish, self-destructive, usually considered a blackguard, but there are reasons for his behaviour. Greasy hair, an earring, and the faded flash of zip-jacket over dirty slacks and plimsolls. Unshaven.

FRANCISCO. . . . Know what I mean? (*MAUDIE's face is blank.*) Alright. Can God do anything? . . . Well, say he can, right? Right. Well, can he make a stone he cannot lift? . . . Okay. You believe in God, right? (*MAUDIE considers it. Then nods.*) Right. God made the world, right? and fair play to him. What has he done since? Tell me. Right, I'll tell you. Evaporated himself. When they painted his toe-nails and turned him into a church he lost his ambition, gave up learning, stagnated for a while, then gave up even that, said fuck it, forget it, and became a vague pain in his own and everybody else's arse. (*MAUDIE laughs at the four letter words.*) Aha, you see! We know each other alright. (*He offers her a drink: she declines.*) Take Jesus. Jesus was A-one. Know what I mean? But they've nearly written him out of existence. He might as well have been Napoleon. As a matter of fact I think that all concerned would have been better off. Supposing the Holy Ghost, or whosoever, had chosen to do a few tricks with old Napoleon Bonaparte, this whole cosmos would be a different kettle of fish. (*Offers drink again: she declines.*) Sure, Maud? I don't think he's (*Harry*) coming back. No, as a fairly experienced punter, in the three horse race of the Trinity, I'm inclined to give my vote to your man, the Holy Spirit. Alias the Friendly Ghost. He's the coming man. Would you agree? But, yes, yes, maybe you're right, because – yes, yes – when you think of it, him being symbolised by a dove and all that, I'm inclined to agree that he was the original bat in the belfry. What? So how are you going to get forgiveness from that lot? Have you ever thought who's going to forgive them? Who's going to forgive the Gods, hmm? (*Laughs.*) So the state they must be in! What? There's no such thing as forgiveness.

MAUDIE. There is.

FRANCISCO. There isn't.

MAUDIE. There is.

FRANCISCO. Hmm? . . . And is Harry looking for forgiveness too? (MAUDIE *shrugs.*) He should be.

MAUDIE. Strength, I think.

FRANCISCO. And I'd like the whole place to fall down. (*In reaction to a smile from her.*) What?

MAUDIE. Not with yourself inside.

FRANCISCO. And singing and dancing and talking to Jesus here and everything? Very nice.

MAUDIE. Not *really* dancing.

FRANCISCO. Not really dancing? Still, very nice. And he's looking for strength? What has he been saying about me? . . . Did he mention what great friends we are? (MAUDIE *shrugs.*) Did he tell you I'm his best friend?

MAUDIE. No.

FRANCISCO. Oh yes: Old Har and I are the last of the Texas Rangers. (*To himself.*) And I have some news for my friend.

The clock chimes one o'clock.

There: one o'clock. I really don't think he's coming back.
What?

MAUDIE. I think he might have gone to buy some fish and
chips.

FRANCISCO. No, I'm telling you, he got the push from the
coonic. So why not come back to my place in Paxton Street?
There's no one else there now. Maud? . . . Well, I'll tell you,
we'll give him another five minutes, okay? Then we'll blow
. . . Cold, isn't it? I find it very hard to be on my own. Find it
very hard to sleep on my own. Do you? (*He has his arm
around her.*)

MAUDIE. What are you doing?

FRANCISCO. Just take my hand then.

MAUDIE (*considers it, then*). No.

FRANCISCO. Okay. (*He lights a cigarette.*) – Oh, do you want
one?

MAUDIE (*considers it, then*). No.

FRANCISCO. I can't sleep sometimes because I can't stop
thinking. Know what I mean?

MAUDIE. I'm always thinking.

FRANCISCO. Yeh? Do you do the trick for him?

MAUDIE. What?

FRANCISCO. Okay. What do you think about?

MAUDIE. . . . Everything.

FRANCISCO. Yeh? I think about all the flesh in the world. And
all the hopes. *And* the prayers. And all the passions of the
passions, in heaps higher than all the cathedrals, burning in a
constant flame. And my own heart, the fuse, keeping things
burning. And if it blows, so does the lot. That's what I think

about. What do you think about? And I'd love to stop
thinking.

MAUDIE. So would I.

FRANCISCO. Yeh? (*She nods.*) Yeh?

MAUDIE. I think about Stephen.

FRANCISCO. Stephen? Another boyfriend?

MAUDIE. A boyfriend? – Stephen! No! Not a boyfriend.

FRANCISCO. Yeh? (*She averts her eyes.*) . . . You have a baby,
Maud? Stephen? Is that who you think about? At night?
Awake and asleep?

MAUDIE. What?

FRANCISCO. Did he die? Did you have him adopted?

MAUDIE. . . . . Shall I tell you?

FRANCISCO. Take my hand. Yeh?

MAUDIE. Do you know – hospitals? Well, my grandad said let
someone else take care of me. Well, I come home late one
night and he were waiting. In the hall. In his bare feet. And
he found eight new p. in my pocket. *I* don't know how it got
there. Maybe one of the bigger boys. And grandad said he
would have kicked me, if he had his boots on. And grandad
said let someone else take care of me to have a baby. And
gran was lucky to find me one of those hospitals. And I had a
baby. I knew he were not well. But I knew if I could not take
care of him, who could? And once I woke and they were
taking him away. And I growled. But there were an old – Do
you know nuns? Well, there were an old nun. She were in
black, the others were in white, and she were my friend. And
she said had I thought of a name for him. *I* hadn't thought of
a name. And she said would I call him Stephen. Because that
were her name. And she would like that. And I said okay. And
they smiled – the way I said 'okay'. And I laughed. But I were
not happy at all. But I were so warm and sleepy. I wanted to

sit up so they'd see I were not happy. Because I were crying. So they took him away to baptize him. Because he were not well. And the next time I woke up, only the old nun were there. And she come to me, sort of smiling and frowning together. And she said 'Maudie. Maudie'. Like that. Like as if I were asleep. But I were awake. I were wide awake. And she said, 'Stephen is dead, Maudie. Stephen is with Jesus'. At first I didn't know if she were only fibbing, but when he started to visit me – No, not dreaming! Not dreaming! So all around me! – I knew he were dead alright. But I didn't tell them. Because I wanted them to let me go. And I didn't want the other patients to pull my hair. I only told the old nun. To ask her would it stop. And she said it would, in time. And I said, when I got forgiveness, was it? And she said yes.

FRANCISCO *feels commiseration but he reacts harshly.*

FRANCISCO. There's no such thing! (MAUDIE *is near tears. She looks at him.*) No such thing. That's not thinking – that's dreaming.

MAUDIE. What? . . . That's what gran said about my mam.

FRANCISCO. Dreaming.

MAUDIE. Then why doesn't it stop?

FRANCISCO. I don't know. Dreaming!

MAUDIE. Is it? . . . And with fair hair and blue eyes.

FRANCISCO. What colour are your eyes?

MAUDIE. Brown.

FRANCISCO ('*There you are then*':). That's it: dreaming.

MAUDIE. Well I just want him to stop. To say he's alright and to stop.

FRANCISCO *sighs.*

FRANCISCO. Night is a funny time, isn't it?

MAUDIE. Is that what you think? (*He nods.*)

FRANCISCO . . . (*gently*). That's dreaming, Maud. (*She looks at him.*) Quite frankly it must be, or else you're daft. (*He smiles. Then she smiles. He laughs, then she laughs.*) When I was young, really young, do you know what I used to think about every night? – What age are you?

MAUDIE. *My* age?

FRANCISCO. You're over sixteen, aren't you?

MAUDIE. I was sixteen on the 21st of February.

FRANCISCO. And what do you do?

MAUDIE. What do *I* do?

FRANCISCO. Yeh. Job.

MAUDIE. *Me*?

FRANCISCO. Yeh.

MAUDIE. *I* don't have a job.

FRANCISCO. And you won't come back to Paxton Street with me? . . . Hmm?

MAUDIE. Did you think I had a job.

FRANCISCO. Yeh. Call me Francisco, Maud. Know what I mean?

MAUDIE. Alright.

They hear HARRY returning. FRANCISCO looks frightened, stubs out his cigarette, then puts a finger to his lips warning MAUDIE to keep silent. FRANCISCO hides. MAUDIE hiding a giggle at this game. HARRY enters by side door (the key he stole earlier). He has a small parcel. Then FRANCISCO is heard singing. HARRY's hand to his pocket for his knife, then decides to play it coolly.

FRANCISCO. 'God of mercy and compassion, look with pity upon me; Father, let me call thee Father, 'tis thy child returns to thee; Jesus Lord, I ask for mercy, let me not implore in vain – ' Harry! (*Coming out of hiding – laughing.*) Jesus Lord! Jesus Lord! (*Sings.*) 'All my sins I now detest them; never will I sin again'. Harry! For what reason have I this fortnight been a banished pal from my friend Harry?

HARRY. Oh, hello, Francisco. That was very – y'know? (*The singing.*) (*He glances at the bottle of wine.*)

FRANCISCO. I took the liberty of helping myself. They owe it to me.

HARRY. Not at all, old boy. I knew you'd show up.

FRANCISCO. What's with the running out on us like that?

HARRY. You're looking very well.

FRANCISCO. What's with the giving me the run around, Hymie? (HARRY *pauses for a moment, then walks past* FRANCISCO *returning to the side door.*) Won't you join me? (*In a drink.*)

HARRY (*exiting*). Not at the moment, old boy. (*We hear* HARRY *off, locking the door.*)

FRANCISCO. What's he doing?

MAUDIE. Locking the door.

HARRY *returns, affecting to ignore* FRANCISCO.

FRANCISCO. Won't you join me? (*Offering wine.*)

HARRY. No thank you. (*He produces fish and chips from his parcel.*)

FRANCISCO. Won't she? (*Have a drink.*) Maud?

HARRY. Quite in order, Maudie – if you wish. Would you like a? Get a cup.

MAUDIE *exits to the sacristy.*

FRANCISCO. Get two cups! . . . She's a big young girl, Har?

HARRY. Oh yes.

FRANCISCO (*a dirty laugh*). Hah?

HARRY. Indeed.

FRANCISCO. Well, it's good to see you, fella!

HARRY. You're looking very well, extremely so, how are you?

FRANCISCO. Terrific. Here comes Maud.

HARRY. I was actually on my way to visit you outside just now but, there you are, I turned back.

MAUDIE *has returned with two cups.* HARRY *pours a cup of wine for her.*

FRANCISCO. Have some, Har.

HARRY. No thank you, old boy.

HARRY *has taken out his penknife to divide the fish between himself and* MAUDIE; *he excludes* FRANCISCO. *Though feigning casualness and affecting to ignore* FRANCISCO, *his movements are tense and deliberate.*

I took the liberty, Maudie, of getting some fish and chips. Not enough money for two pieces and they were actually sold out of cod. But never mind, haddock's very nice too.

MAUDIE. Ta.

FRANCISCO. Not gefülte fish!

HARRY. Very nice, mind you. Just, it hasn't got the same beneficial juices.

FRANCISCO. I was educated – brought up you could say – by the Jesuits. Give me a child until he is seven they say, and then you can have him back! If there's one thing my life disproves it's that. And that's what I aim to go on disproving.

HARRY (*to* MAUDIE *who, he feels, is giving too much attention to* FRANCISCO). Not too much vinegar I hope, Maudie?

MAUDIE (*shakes her head, then to* FRANCISCO). Does Jesus give back the child?

FRANCISCO. Jesuits, Jesuits.

HARRY (*to* MAUDIE). Hmm?

MAUDIE. What's a Jesuit?

FRANCISCO. It is a distortion of a Jesus with sex in the head and tendencies towards violence! (*He laughs.*) I have a dream! I have a dream! The day is coming, the not too distant future! The housewives of the capitals of the world – Yea, the housewives of the very Vatican itself, marching daily to the altar-rails to be administered of the pill at the hands of the Pope himself!

HARRY. Yours alright, Maudie? (*She nods but is inclined to laugh with* FRANCISCO.)

FRANCISCO. Here's one! What's a curate trying to be a parish priest? A mouse trying to be a rat!

HARRY. Not too much salt I hope, Maudie? (*She shakes her head.*)

FRANCISCO. We had this great chat, Har, Maud and me, and she told me all. And I was telling her what great friends we were. Do you know what he did one night? The drinking and carousing in the old days! We came out of this pub and, suddenly, there's Harry with his false teeth in his hand, throws them on the ground and starts dancing on them. 'I'll have nothing false in my head!' Har, remember?

HARRY (*to* MAUDIE). Not too much – too much – y'know?

MAUDIE. No.

FRANCISCO. What's all the cold shoulder for? Do you sleep with women, my son? I doze, father, I doze!

HARRY (*reacts angrily for a moment*). Just a moment, old boy! We're – y'know? – dining. (*Pause.* HARRY *and* MAUDIE *continue eating.*)

FRANCISCO (*Quietly*). Take me to that millionaire in Rome and I'll walk theologically all over him. (*He sits with his arm around* MAUDIE.) Maud and I were nearly going off when you were out. Weren't we? (MAUDIE *giggles*.)

HARRY. What? (*Sharply to* MAUDIE.) And certain things are very naughty – very wicked things to be doing! So – y'know? – eat up, and then the waste, refuse, to be disposed of. Et cetera.

FRANCISCO. What are you talking about?

HARRY. Just a second, old boy. Not too glib now. Remember that movie queen, Maria Del Nostro? I had her.

FRANCISCO. What?

HARRY. I'd just like you all to know that. The ladies always came after me. For sex, actually. Very enjoyable. Y'know? Which is more than can be said for – (Francisco) and – (Olga) Film stars. Very charming. Remember the Irish-American prima donna actually, Chastity O'Casey? (*He nods, meaning he had her too.*) Sixteen years of age. (HARRY *was sixteen.*) My first time.

FRANCISCO. What's with the confession?

HARRY. Took her over the sticks. A hunting lodge, Maudie. And I was up at three, half three and a quarter to four, waiting for tomorrow, waiting for the dawn to go hunting. And whom should I see arriving at the lodge with a member of our party but the goddess – she was goddess actually – Chastity O'Casey. I ran back to my bed, heard them clumping up the stairs, and the member of our party going into the – y'know? – where it was obvious he was being sick. And where a few minutes later he had obviously actually collapsed. Then some moments later my door flew open and in strode the Irish-American prima donna, Chastity O'Casey, and said 'Hey, son, you're doing nothing there, come on'. So, y'see?

FRANCISCO. I remember Chastity O'Casey. Vaguely.

HARRY. They always came looking for me, Maudie. I never had to be sneaky.

FRANCISCO. Who am I sneaking now?

HARRY. Also you're a very bad juggler.

FRANCISCO. Chastity O'Casey: must be dead twenty years now. Some tribes have these rites of initiation: like scourging, tattooing, or knocking out their front teeth. Harry had Chastity O'Casey.

HARRY. Just like you all to know that. I'm not one to brag normally, and I would like to apologise for mentioning the ladies' names in question.

FRANCISCO. I was talking about –

HARRY. Just a second, old boy! More wine, Maudie?

FRANCISCO. Later days.

HARRY. Later days?

FRANCISCO. When we met. We must have been the first pair of Bohemians around these parts. The laughs we had, Har. He had started to go downhill – (HARRY *glances at him.*) slightly. I mean I hadn't even started uphill. Remember the little yellow plastic bucket, Har?

HARRY. No.

FRANCISCO. We had this little yellow plastic bucket, Maud, and we had a bicycle. Me on the carrier with the bucket, and Harry peddling, up and down the road the two of us, always laughing, we'd wash a few cars and we had enough to get by until tomorrow.

HARRY. Don't remember.

FRANCISCO. But, of course, that had to end. My best friend deserted me. Got married, middle-class values, the lot, a little woman.

HARRY. Middle-class values: going back to the circus?

FRANCISCO. Respectability, new shoes –

HARRY. Took you in again –

FRANCISCO. You sent for me!

HARRY. Took you in again, got you a job.

FRANCISCO. But I think it was the new shoes that got me most of all.

HARRY. Took you in, got the sack, lost the lot.

FRANCISCO. Ah, they were not long, those plastic bucket days of wine and roses!

HARRY *stands suddenly*.

HARRY. What do you want?

FRANCISCO. What?

HARRY. I'm not a fool, Francisco! What are all these – memories – about?

FRANCISCO. . . . I just dropped in: for God's sake! (*Then soberly, quietly*.) We could start again. You'll be looking for something new now anyway.

HARRY. Something new?

FRANCISCO. I heard the coonic talking to you.

HARRY. A Monsignor actually. Very decent, very charming.

FRANCISCO. I was listening.

HARRY. I'd like to see someone raise a finger to him.

FRANCISCO. Giving you the sack.

HARRY. Cheekie chappie, he said.

FRANCISCO. Giving you the bullet.

HARRY. I thought you might follow him – I knew you'd show up.

FRANCISCO. He fired you!

HARRY. Oh no.

FRANCISCO. I heard him!

HARRY. Got it wrong.

FRANCISCO (*appeals to her*). Maud!

HARRY. It doesn't change things!

FRANCISCO. It doesn't . . . ?

HARRY. We'll still go on living here!

FRANCISCO. Be realistic!

HARRY. It's all worked out! – We'll still go on – And you will keep the little secret of our residence – Be realistic? – won't you? (FRANCISCO *is now more conscious of the threat and of the penknife in* HARRY's *hand*.)

FRANCISCO. Okay. (*Moving a little away from* HARRY: *he picks up the wine bottle and demonstrates that it is empty. To* MAUDIE.) This altar wine has gone to my head.

HARRY. Put it down. (*The bottle.*)

FRANCISCO (*still talking to* MAUDIE). I'm more accustomed to the humbler 'table' wine.

HARRY. Francisco!

FRANCISCO. You from round here, Maud?

HARRY. Tell him to mind his own –

MAUDI (*to* FRANCISCO). I'm from 32 Rock's Lane. (HARRY *is growing confused by* FRANCISCO's *attitude and by his feeling of* MAUDIE's *shifting allegiance*.)

HARRY. Francisco! – (*Turns to* MAUDIE.) Waste – refuse – Dispose of! (*To* FRANCISCO.) Put it down.

FRANCISCO. Okay. Okay, forget it. (*Puts down the bottle. He is moving away.*)

HARRY. Where do you think you're going?

FRANCISCO (*stops*). Another bottle of bourgeois.

HARRY. Just a moment. (HARRY *goes to* FRANCISCO *and sends him sprawling with a punch.*) Now can we be civil?

FRANCISCO. Aw, for fuck's sake! What's the matter with you? (HARRY *is coming for him again.*) I've something to tell you! (HARRY *hits him again, flattening him this time.*)

HARRY. See him! See him! See him, Maudie! So I'm not as – y'know? – dilapidated as you might think. Now, why do you give everyone in the world a hard time?

FRANCISCO. Well, this one for the book.

HARRY. What?

FRANCISCO. A half-lapsed Jew here –

HARRY. Francisco!

FRANCISCO. In residence –

HARRY. Francisco!

FRANCISCO. A Catholic church, with a young chick.

HARRY. Or I shall have to make the other ear pop. See him! Not so cocky as he was. Not so cocky as when last I saw you. Yes, get another bottle of wine, Maudie. (*She does not move.*) Get it! (*She goes.*) Do Olga and Sam know I'm here? . . . Do you hear me, Francisco?

FRANCISCO. I don't know.

HARRY. What?

FRANCISCO. No. God only knows how many sacrileges you've committed here!

HARRY. Oh no.

FRANCISCO. Yes!

HARRY. You believe in nothing, so, as far as you're concerned I've committed nothing, see? (MAUDIE *returns with a bottle of wine which* HARRY *uncorks, etc.*) See him? You have nothing, Francisco. You, Olga, or Sam. I always believed in things. And when you have nothing and you believe in nothing, you have nothing at all!

FRANCISCO. Oh, I have a few things.

HARRY. Like what, for instance?

FRANCISCO (*his face expressing his loathing and impotence*). Oh, I have a few things.

HARRY. Like my wife for instance? How is she? Hmm? Do – you – hear – me?

FRANCISCO. Fine. (HARRY *chuckles.*)

HARRY. And those little plastic bucket days: just a few years for me, interim actually. (*He takes a slug from the new bottle of wine, then places it near* FRANCISCO.) Your wine, Francisco. Something to tell me? (FRANCISCO *takes a drink. Through the following his attitude swings from artifice to abandon.*)

FRANCISCO (*mutters*). I've something to tell you alright.

HARRY. What did you say?

FRANCISCO. Unless you resolve to suffer and die things will not get better says the Lord! Speak up, speak up, Lord, your servant is listening! So, you've found yourself here, Har, have you? You find yourself here too, Maud? And I lost myself in a place like this.

HARRY. Have you something to tell me?

FRANCISCO. Yeh? Can I top up yours, Maud? Can I top up hers, Har? (*Sexual innuendo/gesture with the bottle. He laughs harshly.*)

HARRY. Francisco!

FRANCISCO (*harshly*). Yes, Har! What I was looking for you for, was to tell you how that last engagement went. The one you walked out on. The biggest engagement we ever got and he disappeared. Sidon, blush for shame, says the sea!

HARRY. Yes?

FRANCISCO. You're interested, are you?

HARRY. Must confess: trifle curious.

FRANCISCO. Yeh? Well, hang on. Cheers! (*He drinks again.*) Well that final gig. *And* its consequences.

HARRY. Did you not get another engagement since then? (HARRY *is pleased.*)

FRANCISCO. Yeh? Yes, I can see that you're happy here in the bosom of blind old Abraham. But that last engagement: No doubt it was an experience not to be missed. And – *and* – they didn't ask old Olga to do a strip: I bet that will surprise you. Does that not surprise you? Har?

HARRY (*uncomfortable*). Oh yes?

FRANCISCO. Oh, sorry – sorry! – sorry for talking shop, love. Has he not told you about our line of business? Have you not told her about – ? Hmm?

HARRY. No.

FRANCISCO. What! Did you not see our ad in *The Times*? 'All the thrills of the circus, live in your drawingroom'. And whose idea do you think it was? (*Points at* HARRY.) The very man. The celebrity. (HARRY *makes some move, looking dangerous.*) Well, we all contributed. So maybe we are all to blame.

HARRY. Blame?

FRANCISCO. So long as we could perform.

HARRY. What blame?

FRANCISCO. The showman must go on – Right Har? This
senseless desire that *some* of us had to please. And be liked.

HARRY. What are you on about?

FRANCISCO. We were on a good thing. Not many
engagements but forty nicker a time when we got them. And
for that last engagement, well, with just three of us, we
demanded only thirty.

HARRY. Francisco –

FRANCISCO. I just want to explain to Maud, and to Jesus
there. (*The lamp.*) Cause she told me all. But the perks were
always good, weren't they, Har? Har?

HARRY. Oh yes.

FRANCISCO. We got the grub. Free gargle. Why, the most
VSOP ten-year-old Napoleon Bonapartes for him always.
And we'd nick some grub, nick some sauce. And you know
this two-and-a-half foot friend of ours, Maud? Do you know
the first thing little Sam would do on a Saturday night
engagement? Check the hostess's fridge for our Sunday joint!
Oh, a very carnally-minded little man was Sam. Right, Har?
(HARRY *cautious, vigilant, but amused.*) And do you know
how he'd get it out? Smuggle it out, by using it as a hump!

HARRY. Aw, Francisco! –

FRANCISCO. And needless to say, no one ever searches a
dwarf.

HARRY. Don't you believe him. (*He chuckles.*)

FRANCISCO. Clever?

HARRY. Aw, Francisco.

FRANCISCO (*smiling humourlessly*). What, Har? (HARRY
*remembering that the situation is not funny; his penknife held
up to remind* FRANCISCO *that he has got him where he
wants him.* FRANCISCO *nods.*) But to return to Olga, Olga,
Olga. Well, why not, in answer to the calls of a world in

search of sensation shouldn't a good-natured husband and a philosophical best man allow her to strip? Y'know – y'know – y'know! What, Har? – Sorry, Har? – I didn't hear, Har? And, Maud, post-striptease at our engagements, the host was always allowed to chat old Olga up, for the slice. Know what I mean? And, or, optionally, alternatively, one or two other selected guests. This senseless desire we had to please, you see? And be liked. (HARRY's *head is bowed.* FRANCISCO *is watching him.*) Oh we were a band intimate! (FRANCISCO *tip-toes away and hides in the pulpit.* HARRY *becomes aware of the silence and looks about for* FRANCISCO.)

HARRY. Francisco!

FRANCISCO (*shows himself in the pulpit*). Don't let your soul suffer from neglect!

HARRY. Come down!

FRANCISCO. But the pattern of man's sins will be the pattern of his punishment! See the depraved ones, who so loved their own pleasures, now bathing in black, hot, bubbling pitch and reeking sulphur! See the gluttonous pigs, now parched and hungry! –

HARRY. Come down! –

FRANCISCO. And what of the tardy-footed giants who did not lift a finger? See them: masters of sorrow, go howling like dogs for very grief! Do you want absolution, Har?

HARRY. Come down!

HARRY *is coming towards* FRANCISCO. FRANCISCO *pulls up the little ladder which leads to the pulpit – or uses candlestick, as below.*

FRANCISCO. Know what I mean, Har? The ones who didn't lift a finger – but who now claim they know better. (HARRY *starts to lurch at the pulpit and* FRANCISCO *produces a candlestick which he can obviously use as a weapon.*) Y'know

– y'know – y'know! There was no one but myself to kiss away the tears of that poor, unhappy, lost, unfaithful wife.

HARRY. And Teresa?

FRANCISCO. Yes.

HARRY. And Teresa!

FRANCISCO. Everyone to blame but you, Har?

HARRY rushes in, under the pulpit, and with a mighty effort lifts it off its base.

Hup! Hup! Voilà!

HARRY. See! See!

HARRY lets the pulpit down. He is panting, doubled up, after his effort, but is proud of his achievement.

FRANCISCO. Bravo!

HARRY. See! See! Come down now, Francisco.

FRANCISCO. Something to tell you, Har. Y'know – y'know – y'know!

HARRY. Alright, I can wait.

FRANCISCO. I haven't told you about that last engagement yet.

HARRY (*to* MAUDIE). See?

FRANCISCO. *And* its consequences.

In the foregoing and in the following there is a strange import in FRANCISCO's *references to* OLGA *which makes* HARRY *pause – but only fleetingly:* HARRY *keeps banishing the thought that* OLGA, *too, is dead. The clock chimes the half hour.* FRANCISCO *goes through the motions of checking the time on an imaginary pocket watch and placing it in front of him.*

FRANCISCO. My dear brethren in Christ, the story of the critic's ball. Or, is there not always a kind of melancholy attaching to the glory we attain in this world? Some of you are no doubt aware of a certain troupe who were called upon one evening to tender service, and sow the seeds of merriment at the mansion of a mighty man who writes only for the most important papers and who even has his own television show. Why, it was said of this man that he could turn an artist into a cult. Didn't we say that, Har?

HARRY. Not a dirty story now, Francisco —

FRANCISCO. No — no — no. Anyways, as Harry says, we got to the place —

HARRY. Really got you where I want you now, Francisco.

FRANCISCO (*nods, agreeing*). There were two large rooms adjoining for the party. One for the intellectuals, drink-sipping and telling dirty stories, the other for drink-slopping, dancing, and groping, which I think they call goosing. There were people there from all nations. The mandatory one black was there of course, T.V. personalities, people from the press, jilly-journalists — Don't be talking! — talking about appliances, perversions, performances, their faces sexually awake as currant buns. And so on. It was our big break.

    Well, we performed and, truth to tell, it was not of our best. (HARRY *chuckles*.) Yes, I'll admit that. Howandever, Har, I'm glad to say that when we were through, the intellectuals would have nothing but our joining them in their very own room. And you know how nobody ever touches a dwarf? Well, I'm glad to say that as we stood 'round in an obedient circle, our champagne glasses to attention, Sam stood proudly at the great man's leg, the great man's fingers, stiff as pencils, gently resting on Sam's shoulder. Oh, the great man knew your name, Har, and of your erstwhile fame, and many were the regrets expressed at your inability to be among us.

HARRY. Oh yes?

FRANCISCO. But we were enjoying ourselves. And why not? And everyone was secretly congratulating himself on fitting in so well in such manifest civilization. And one wondered what could possibly go wrong.

Well, in the most civilized of manners, Olga, not in our circle, but following the usual pattern that we'd all agreed upon, was smiling 'cross the crowded room at our host and employer. Whose expression betrayed the double-meaning that he would not have minded the slice at all, but that he found something in old Olga a trifle frightening. So, the seignorial right was waived and, to make a long story shorter, a first sub, an impetuous, squat and sweaty standby led old Olga to the kitchen where, tugging at his zip, he tried to have her half way on-and-off the Sir Basil Wedgewood kitchen table. It was then of course that Madame Standby, his good wife, made an unfortunate and untimely entrance – unfortunate for herself that is. For she was incapable of throwing more than a look of outrage in such a circumstance. For which silent pacifism she received a puck in the eye from her hubby, the Lord of the flies. Meanwhile, harmony is continuing at the party proper. Our host still smiling and showing his fillings, his famous hand still favouring the lucky Sam. It was then I saw old Olga returning from her domestic adventure and I knew by the look she threw our way that her party piece was coming. You know it, you know it, Har, as well as anyone. 'People – people – I hate them – Just look at them.'

HARRY. 'Haven't you seen them riding bicycles?'

FRANCISCO. That's it. Of course our host is clocking all these new developments too, and the further development a moment later of Madame Standby's reappearance from the kitchen, her eye already swelling up. And to follow this, the re-entry of her randy spouse, who was now, for reasons best known to himself, pretending to be chewing gum. Well, that did it. Well, it must have. Because it was then, suddenly, in mid-anecdote, that the famous favouring hand was withdrawn, and the deep rich resonant voice said sternly

down at Sam, 'I'm afraid I must ask you to leave.' 'Pardon?'
said Sam. From his vantage point he had been clocking
nothing, so his amazement was clearly understandable.
'Pardon?' he said again, and I thought he was going to faint.
'Leave, leave, leave!' screamed the great man shrilly, revealing
that the deep rich resonance all along was – falsetto. And,
simultaneously, as I'm seeing out of the corner of my eye, the
randy Monsieur Standby hurrying 'cross the crowded room
bent on doing me a damage, I got a puck in the back from
another quarter which sent me sprawling towards our host.
'Just a moment, please' – I was very polite – but the next
thing, I was looking at a fistful of my hair in the hand that
could turn an artist into a cult. Nor could the great man
himself believe the sight of the fistful of my hair – so what
was his reaction? – but to attempt to get another and
another.

HARRY *laughs*.

Enjoying it so far, Har?
    In short, it was a vicious intellectual do. Actually, it was
Sam who cleared the space which allowed me to pull free and
see three heroes paw and grapple with old Olga, lift her off
her feet – their excited arms and hands were to-and-fro her
clutch – and bear her out the screaming door. Everyone was
excited. They would not of course touch Sam, and for this
very reason he was to-and-fro – particularly the screaming
jilly-journalists – kicking them mercilessly in their fast-
growing hysterical shins, and causing spaces. Actually, it was
by means of one of these spaces that I made my escape,
leaving – Mea Culpa! – little Sam behind. Well, they would
have killed *me*! They would! They were intellectuals and
therefore only half-wide. They could kill you, so little do they
know about it all. They would really hurt you.
    But eventually they got Sam out too. With walking sticks
they did it. Not to beat him, no! As I said they were loath to
even touch him. Loath to! To knock him. Hook his little legs,
knock, haul, prod – encourage him to leave. Hmm? What a
regrettable *volte-face* for civilization, I said to myself a

thousand times, and did not God, through his only begotten son, his *only* son — because He had only the one — redeem us from all this kind of thing. Could I have a drink, Har?

HARRY (*taking bottle to* FRANCISCO). Y'see? Y'see?

FRANCISCO. Have one yourself, Har.

HARRY. Without me you are nothing. (*Gives bottle to* FRANCISCO.)

FRANCISCO. Are you quoting Scripture now?

HARRY. You were being punished.

FRANCISCO. Oh?

HARRY. And soon you will be punished more.

FRANCISCO. By you?

HARRY. Yes, by me. And then by God. God found evil among the angels and he didn't spare them, so what will he do with you?

FRANCISCO. So proud, Har, so righteous! What makes you so sure of yourself? Time and time again, people have been caught out. How often have you been told how, in a simple conversation such as this, such a man was stabbed, how such a man fell down and broke his neck, how another never rose from his game of poker? How such a woman killed herself. Hmm? I would have imagined that at this stage you would be saying, what is the point of all this to me. Hmm? (*He is handing the bottle down to* HARRY.)

HARRY. . . . No — no, you keep it, old boy.

FRANCISCO. No, you keep it — old boy. (HARRY, *unsure, takes the bottle, then holds it up to* FRANCISCO *again*.) No, you keep it. I haven't finished yet. (*To* MAUDIE.) Sorry for the deviation, love. What a night of adventure! And all the time I knew – I knew – I knew – I knew, I knew we had not been paid!

HARRY. You didn't get paid!

FRANCISCO. No. But the pain of that thought, Harry. My honour – *my* honour! – exposed and scalding me. But my head would have none of it, and had already told my honour that it could not afford its pride. So, there we were, we three on the outside, looking at the cream-white luxury of that closed apartment door. Olga . . . Yes, contrary to what some people thought, I had a great regard for old Olga.

HARRY. What?

FRANCISCO (*savagely*). Yes Har? (HARRY *mutters something.*) What, Har?

HARRY. I'm not a fool, Francisco.

FRANCISCO (*nods, agreeing*). Olga was trembling, rather sexily I thought, her raven hair in rather lovely disarray, and kept hissing with passionate intensity the one word, cunts, repeatedly at a spot on the door. And Sam, Har – (*Savagely.*) Har!

HARRY. Oh, yes?

FRANCISCO (*controlled*). Sam, also understandably agitated, but making as little constructive sense as Olga, was calling for our concerted effort to 'kick the fucking door down, man, and take the fucking lot of them.' Well, I went to the letterbox, sir, pushed open the flap, and called out the simple message, 'Our money, our money'. I could see them in the hall. What a ripple of excitement was now running through the party! What existentialism! And they called in urgent whispers for the host. I saw the great man appear and with a flourishing biro write us out a cheque on the hall's Sir Basil Wedgewood cheque-book table. I saw his adam's apple bob twice, and to cover this, the only crack in his composure, he kept blowing on the biro-written cheque as he came to the waiting letterbox. He posted me the cheque with eyes cast down – like a Christian. Har – and said 'Be off with you, my man, at once or I shall have the fuzz here in a thrice'. Well, Olga grabbed the cheque to see if we were to be short-changed. But no! It was written out for forty-five, written and printed. Not the thirty nicker we'd agreed upon, but fiften nicker extra. It wasn't a mistake. But as Olga said, why not twenty extra if he wanted to be generous, why not short-change us if he wanted to be a man? If an apology, why not the rounder figure, fifty? Or, as Olga said, is fifteen, three fivers, the standard sum for an insult to three persons? Or is fifteen the figure of an apology for the half man and the phony? Or, in that kind of contingency, as Olga said, is that the sum of Christian charity and amendment? How old Olga wrestled with the psychological apologetics of that one! How that detail preyed on old Olga's mind . . . to the end.

HARRY (*taking bottle to him*). And what did you do?

FRANCISCO. I beg your pardon? (FRANCISCO *is frowning, incredulous of* HARRY's *unwillingness or inability to get the message.*)

HARRY. Did you take it?

FRANCISCO. I thought the tragic ending to my story was lucid.

HARRY. I wouldn't have taken it! I wouldn't, I wouldn't! . . . What? . . . Well I would have . . .

FRANCISCO. Yeh?

HARRY. Well, that's very – y'know? That's very interesting. And what am I expected to do about it? Is it my affair? (*Shouts.*) It's got nothing to do with me!

FRANCISCO. Shh!

HARRY. What?

FRANCISCO (*indicates that somebody outside might hear them. Then:*). It has.

HARRY. What? What did you come here for, Francisco? Francisco, I know you! Do you know what's been going on in my mind for you? (*His knife clutched in his hand.*) And you, Olga, and Sam: I can't take any more of you! You made your filthy bed, now sleep in it. That's a proverb, isn't it? Well then! You – you three make a right – a right Holy Family – A right-looking Holy Family, Maudie! You should see them: Polluting, poisoning the air. So – y'know? – If you'll drink up – If you'd care to drink up, you can be – Toddle along.

FRANCISCO. Oh no.

HARRY. Yes! You can go, leave!

FRANCISCO. I've no intention of going!

HARRY. Stop! I said you can go now.

FRANCISCO. I'm not going traipsing all the way back to Paxton Street –

HARRY. I'm letting you go! –

FRANCISCO. At this hour of the morning.

HARRY. Francisco!

FRANCISCO. Are you a Catholic, Maud?

HARRY. Francisco!

FRANCISCO. Maud –

HARRY. No, she's not.

FRANCISCO. What?

HARRY. She's not, she's not! – Why should she? – Why should she?

FRANCISCO. I agree – How I agree! Don't I agree! What a poxy con the lot is!

HARRY (*wearily*). Francisco.

MAUDIE. I think my mam were.

FRANCISCO. And so was Olga, Maud. And so was Olga, Har.
And I was a Catholic for the F.B.I. But what a con! I knew
you were only joking about being happy here. What an
industry! The great middle-man industry! I had occasion the
other day to negotiate with them, not too successfully, for a
holy grave. But what a poxy con! All Christianity! All those
predators that have been mass-produced out of the loneliness
and isolation of people, with standard collars stamped on!
And what do they give back? Those coonics! They're like
black candles, not giving, but each one drawing a little more
light of the world. (HARRY *makes some movement. A weary
plea to* FRANCISCO: FRANCISCO *misinterprets the move
and swings the candlestick viciously*.) Oh, they could kill you
– Oh they can really hurt you, so little do they know about it
all! Hopping on their rubber-soled formulas and equations!
Selling their product: Jesus. Weaving their theological
cobwebs, doing their theological sums! Black on the outside
but, underneath, their bodies swathed in bandages – bandages
steeped in ointments, preservatives and holy oils! – Half
mummified torsos like great thick bandaged pricks! Founded
in blood, continued in blood, crusaded in blood, inquisitioned
in blood, divided in blood – And *they* tell *us* that Christ lives!
Nothing to live for but to die! They arrive at their temporary
sated state, these violence-mongering furies, and start verily
wanking themselves in pleasurable swoons of pacifism,
forgetting their own history. And then insist – Insist! – that
Jesus, total man, life-enchancing man, Jesus! – should be the
only killer of life! Die to self? I doze father, I doze! Peace,
Ecumenism? – I doze, father, I doze! They cannot agree
among themselves on the first three words of the Our Father!
Get the police in! – (*He laughs.*) Get heavy mounted police in
with heavy mounted batons and disperse them, rout them, get
them back from the round tables before they start the third
and final world war we've all been dreading!

HARRY (*again determined*). Come down!

FRANCISCO *laughs and swings the candlestick viciously
again. The clock chimes two.*

FRANCISCO. I have a dream, I have a dream! The day is coming, the second coming, the final judgment, the not too distant future, before that simple light of man: when Jesus, Man, total man, will call to his side the goats — 'Come ye blessed!' Yea, call to his side all those rakish, dissolute, suicidal, fornicating goats, taken in adultery and what-have-you. And proclaim to the coonics, blush for shame, you blackguards, be off with you, you wretches, depart from me ye accursed complicated affliction! And that, my dear brother and sister, is my dream, my hope, my vision and my belief. (*He comes down from the pulpit and kneels on one knee before* HARRY.) Your blessing, Har.

HARRY (*knife in his hand*). Would you — would you die for your belief?

FRANCISCO (*indicates that he is already kneeling*). You kill for yours? (*Short pause. Rising.*) Then put away your sword. Where do I sleep? Just point to the spot and I'll flop there. We might as well get a few hours before we're evicted.

HARRY (*feebly*). What have you to tell me, Francisco?

FRANCISCO. Aw, you're not that slow on the uptake, Har. Where's the loo? In here, Maud, is it?

MAUDIE *leads* FRANCISCO *off.*

HARRY (*calls after them*). It's Teresa I'm talking about, Teresa! Not Olga . . . 'Everyone to blame but you, Har?' I'm not in the wrong. (*To lamp.*) Do you believe what he says? That muck? All that insinuation? I'm not in the wrong. Did he sneak my wife or didn't he? Well then! Did Teresa die or didn't she? . . . Are you dumb, are you dumb? I was one of the best of sports, anyone will tell you that. I was a famous man. So — y'see? . . . I don't *feel* I'm in the wrong . . . And once, in the morning actually, towards the end, little girl — y'know? — got out of her cot, out of her cot, all by herself — I was very surprised — some music was playing, and danced, actually. Danced. (*He has been weaving his hands in the air, vaguely balletic, reminiscent of a child.*) Of course Olga was a

dancer too. Not a very good one, of course. (*Reconsiders.*)
Well, perhaps above the average. She's gone and left him.
Olga – y'know? That's what I think. That's all . . . (*He is
near tears.*) Are you dumb? . . . I believe . . . Help.

*Music has come up and the lights are fading a little (to
suggest the passage of time). MAUDIE has entered to stand
beside HARRY with an armful of cushions. HARRY rises
wearily to lay the confessional horizontal on the floor.
FRANCISCO from the background coming to his
assistance . . .*

Scene Two

MAUDIE *is asleep in one of the three compartments of the
confessional. FRANCISCO is in another compartment, sitting
up, rolling a cigarette. HARRY is sitting listlessly in a pew. It is
nearly three a.m.*

FRANCISCO (*whispering*). Harry? Harry? . . . Maud? . . .
Maud? (MAUDIE *is waking up.* FRANCISCO *chuckling and
lighting his cigarette.*) Give me a child until he is seven, they
say, and then you can have him back. Ask me to say the
Confiteor. I can't. I've forgotten it. I've beaten them . . .
You're praying to a dying horse here, Har.

HARRY. And what are you doing, kicking him?

FRANCISCO. Not bad. But you agree the horse is dying?

HARRY. No. I don't agree with you.

MAUDIE. You don't get children back. They're gone. You get
other ones.

FRANCISCO. Yeh, they're gone. And there's no one on earth
to tell you where they've gone. And there's no one to bless
you. And, worse, there's no one to curse you.

MAUDIE. There's forgiveness.

FRANCISCO. What? . . . You're free tomorrow, Maud, I'm free too. Know what I mean?

MAUDIE. I'm going home to gran. And to grandad. (*MAUDIE settles back to sleep in her compartment. Pause.*)

FRANCISCO. Teresa, Olga, and Stephen. Dead. Harry, Olga is dead. Two days after that last gig. An overdose. OD. They talked about it in shorthand (*The clock chimes three. HARRY reacts to the clock. He gets the replacement candle for the sanctuary lamp through the following.*) A couple of days later Sam packed his bag. He got taken back into the circus. I tried them too but they wouldn't have me — (*Chuckles.*) for some reason or other . . . Remember the talking we used to do in bed in the old days?

HARRY. Don't remember.

FRANCISCO. The little pad we used to doss in?

HARRY. No.

FRANCISCO. That pad: one big bed. Nothing queer, Maud.

HARRY. Oh, no.

FRANCISCO. Hmm?

HARRY. Nothing like that — y'know?

FRANCISCO. I think she's asleep. We used to sit up in bed half the night talking.

HARRY. Discussing, actually.

FRANCISCO. Yeh.

HARRY. We didn't always agree.

FRANCISCO. But we had a laugh.

HARRY. Excuse for just a second, old boy.

HARRY *replaces the candle in the sanctuary lamp. A touch of ceremony about it all. He returns and sits on a corner of the confessional. They have talked themselves sober.*

I disagree.

FRANCISCO. Yeh?

HARRY. Where you go when you die.

FRANCISCO. Yeh?

HARRY. Silhouettes.

FRANCISCO. Yeh?

HARRY. The soul – y'know? – like a silhouette. And when you die it moves out into . . . slow-moving mists of space and time. Awake in oblivion actually. And it moves out from the world to take its place in the silent outer wall of eternity. The wall that keeps all those moving mists of time and space together.

FRANCISCO. But there must be an outer wall there already.

HARRY. Oh yes. Shell-like.

FRANCISCO. But the wall is built already, if it's an eternal wall.

HARRY. Oh yes.

FRANCISCO. So what's to be done with the new soul – silhouettes that arrive? (*Chuckles.*) Stack them in sheds.

HARRY. No.

FRANCISCO. Yeh?

HARRY. Stack them, softly, like clouds, in a corner of space, where they must wait for a time. Until they are needed.

FRANCISCO. Yeh?

HARRY. And if a hole comes in one of the silhouettes already in that wall, a new one is called for, and implanted on the damaged one. And whose silhouette is the new one? The father's. The father of the damaged one. Or the mother's, sometimes. Or a brother's, or a sweetheart's. Loved ones. That's it. And one is implanted on the other. And the merging – y'know? Merging? – merging of the silhouettes is true union. Union forever of loved ones, actually.

FRANCISCO. I don't know if I agree.

HARRY. Oh yes?

FRANCISCO. But it's certainly as good, better, than anything they've come up with.

HARRY. Oh yes.

FRANCISCO. There was one thing that used to appeal to me. When I was young, Har, do you know what I used to think of every night? The pain of the thought! That I hadn't died before they got to baptize me.

HARRY. Oh yes.

FRANCISCO. Because if you were baptized you could get to heaven alright, but you couldn't get to Limbo.

HARRY. You were disbarred.

FRANCISCO. Yeh. Baptism – the passport to heaven – disbarred you. And contrary to what they thought, I thought – same as any other sensible baby would – that Limbo was the place to get to. It was tropical really. Imagine, the only snag to Limbo was that you never got to see the face of God. Imagine that. Now, what baby, I ask you, gives a burp about the face of God. No, the only thing that babies feared was the hand of God, that could hold your little baby body in his fist, before dipping you into the red hot coals of hell. Then take you out again and hold you up before his unshaved and slobbering chin, before dipping you again, this time into the damp black heat of purgatory. Experimenting. Playing with Himself. Wondering which type of heat to cook you on.

HARRY. Oh yes?

FRANCISCO. No, babies are wide, Har, babies are shrewd. Well, they aren't fools. And they are grossly abused in the great trade-union of Baptism. Oh but Limbo, Har, Limbo! With just enough light rain to kep the place lush green, the sunshine and red flowers, and the thousands and thousands of other fat babies sitting under the trees, gurgling and laughing and eating bananas.

HARRY. . . . Any thoughts on madness, Francisco? . . . No?

FRANCISCO. No, I don't think it's a refuge. Do you?

HARRY. No, actually. No.

FRANCISCO. But that soul-silhouette theory isn't bad. I mean, it's a starting point, you can be developing on it.

HARRY. Indeed.

FRANCISCO. What time have we to be up and out of here?

HARRY. Seven.

FRANCISCO (*he looks at* HARRY *for a moment*). We'll go together, right? (HARRY *nods. Sleepily.*) It's quite an adventure though. It isn't half bad down here. (*Yawns, settling back to sleep.*) Oh my God I am heartily sorry for having offended thee and I . . . See? I can't remember. I've beaten them. Goodnight, Har.

Pause.

HARRY. Y'know!

The Gigli Concert

The Gigli Concert was first performed at the Abbey Theatre, Dublin on Thursday, 29 September 1983 with the following cast:

JPW KING	Tom Hickey
IRISH MAN	Godfrey Quigley
MONA	Kate Flynn

Directed by Patrick Mason
Designed by Bronwen Casson with Frank Hallinan Flood
Lighting by Tony Wakefield

This new version of *The Gigli Concert* was first performed on Tuesday, 19 March 1991 at the Abbey Theatre, Dublin with the following cast:

JPW KING	Tom Hickey
IRISH MAN	Tony Doyle
MONA	Ingrid Craigie

Directed by Patrick Mason
Designed by Monica Frawley
Lighting by Tony Wakefield

The British première of the play was on 3 January 1992 at the Almeida Theatre, London with the following cast:

JPW KING	Barry Foster
IRISH MAN	Tony Doyle
MONA	Ruth McCabe

Directed by Karel Reisz
Designed by Ashley Martin-Davis
Lighting by Alan Burrett

The action is set in JPW King's office which is also his living quarters.

Note

The aria 'Tu che a Dio spiegasti l'ali' on page 229 is the Pearl recording with Gigli, bass and chorus; the same aria on page 239 is a different Pearl recording: Gigli, solo voice (without bass and chorus). The IRISH MAN'S 'Ida' story, pages 208–10, is embraced by 'Toselli's Serenade'. In the trio from 'Attila' – 'Tu sol quest anima' – page 235, the opening soprano solo is to be associated with MONA, the tenor solo with JPW's action, and the following bass solo to be timed with IRISH MAN'S entrance and associated with his action.

For Bennan

Scene One

Beniamino Gigli's voice, distorted, hanging in the air, waiting (to be discovered?), singing 'O Paradiso', mingling with the traffic noise that rises from the street outside. And becoming lost eventually.

A table lamp with a red shade, switched on, and a shaft of yellow light from the washroom, off. JPW comes out of the washroom and goes to his desk. His appearance complements his dingy surroundings (not yet clearly defined). He is English, upper-middle-class, tempering his accent at times – rare – with an Irish intonation and some Irishisms.

He is scraping the remains of a pot of jam on to a piece of bread, then washing it down – his breakfast – with a careful measure from the remains of a bottle of vodka. He interrupts this business to make some illegal adjustment to the telephone connection-box on the wall, then his intense concentration, rapping out a number on his telephone with the edge of his hand. (His rapping is illegal phone-tapping: all this is a recurring action when he wants to use the phone.) His vulnerability, waiting, holding his breath.

JPW. Me . . . Fine . . . Is it? . . . Yes, usually sunny after . . . Yes, and crisp . . . after frost . . . No, I'm still here . . . Same answer I suppose? (*Silently.*) Please . . . (*He nods solemnly to her reply.*) . . . 'Bye . . . What? . . . No, I shan't phone you again . . . I promise . . . I promise . . . 'Bye.

He goes to the window and lets up the blind. Morning light into the room defining the set. Faded lettering on the street-side of the window 'JPW KING – DYNAMATOLOGIST'. He stands looking out over the roofs of the city.

Christ, how am I going to get through today?

The office is dingy, cluttered. A bed that converts into a couch, a desk – hugely cluttered – with a telephone, a kettle; filing cabinet, clothes about the place, books, dusty charts on a wall and a photograph of 'Steve'; another wall and door in frosted-glass panels, flowers withering in a vase, an old leather bag (suitcase) . . .

A ring of a bell on an outer door. A second and third ring. JPW becoming conscious, wary. Into action: readjustment to telephone connection-box. Outer door opening and the silhouette of IRISH MAN in the next room, outside the frosted-glass panels. IRISH MAN knocking at door.

JPW. Yes?

IRISH MAN. Mr King?

JPW. Who is it? . . . Who is that?

IRISH MAN. Can I come in?

JPW. Pardon?

IRISH MAN. To talk.

JPW. To what?

IRISH MAN (*muffled*). To sing.

JPW. What did you say? . . . What did he say? To what? . . . Bloody hell!

Breakfast things into drawers, bed – as best he can – reconverted to couch, too late to shave, but spectacles from somewhere for effect. He unlocks the glass-panelled door which leads to an anteroom.

Yes?

IRISH MAN. Mr King?

JPW. What?

IRISH MAN. Can I come in?

JPW. What do you want?

IRISH MAN. Ah . . . (*He comes in.*)

JPW. There is possibly some mistake, Mr – Mr. (*Off, a church clock chiming the half hour.*) Half-twelve?

IRISH MAN. Eleven.

JPW. I must get the lock on that (*Outer.*) door mended.

The IRISH MAN, *though with head bowed, is taking in the dingy room. JPW assessing* IRISH MAN: *the expensive respectable dress, top coat, silk scarf, gloves, hat (hat a little out of keeping: 30s–40s American style – as worn by Gigli) and* IRISH MAN's *hand in his pocket, quietly toying with something – a recurring action – it could be a gun.*

IRISH MAN. I . . .

JPW. Yes?

IRISH MAN. . . . happened to see your sign as I was passing.

JPW. What sign?

IRISH MAN. Are you the? (*He nods at the lettering on the window.*)

JPW. Dynamatologist.

IRISH MAN. JPW King.

JPW. I have the letters before my name.

IRISH MAN. You were letting up the blind.

JPW. Well, actually, I have been meaning to have that sign – removed?

IRISH MAN. I read something about you.

JPW. Me?

IRISH MAN. Your organisation.

JPW. Anything good?

IRISH MAN. Well, it was a few years ago. In the papers.

JPW. Personally, I thought that article a bit unfair myself.
Hmm?

IRISH MAN *nods*.

I mean to say, water off my back as far as I am . . . You have
not come about? (*The telephone.*) Have you come to consult
me?

IRISH MAN *considering* JPW.

I mean to say.

IRISH MAN. Yes. (*Or an ambiguous nod.*)

JPW. Well, that's different. Yes, if you would care to? (*Sit.*) As
you please. But lest there should be some misunderstanding, I
should say at the outset that dynamatology is not a military
oriented movement. Self-realisation, you know? Because I had
another caller, a gentleman of enquiring intellect,
undoubtedly, yes, but had misinterpreted our meaning, in a
trench-coat. Hmm? (IRISH MAN *nods*.) I knew that. As
Steve puts it, mind is the essence of being alive. Steve our
founder and leader. Revolutionary thinker.

IRISH MAN. It said in the papers –

JPW. Water off my back: wanting us banned in Britain.

IRISH MAN. About ye saying anything is possible.

JPW. That is what I am explaining. The emphasis they put on
the brain. But what is brain? Biological matter, meat. Mind is
the essence. Yes?

IRISH MAN. I haven't much time for philosophy.

JPW. Busy man, aren't we all.

IRISH MAN. No. I've all the time in the world – if I want it.

JPW. Check. Your simple notion of life as substance is useful, I
dare say, but we have gone beyond the macroscopic level into
the subatomic world, and substance is simply – nonsense.
Atoms, my friend. Atoms consist of whirlings – you may call

them particles but we call them whirlings – and whirlings are not made of – anything. But what are our whirlings presently doing? In layman's terms, dancing with each other, and that is an awful waste of energy. So what are we to do? Process of destratification until we arrive at that state we call Nihil where we can start putting our little dancers to proper work, and working properly they can go a very long way indeed to project you beyond the boundaries that are presently limiting you. Now you have a question.

IRISH MAN. How much?

JPW. Pardon?

IRISH MAN. Your fees.

JPW. Fees can wait. *The* priority, a good relationship of trust, mutual feed of energy between auditor – that's me – and subject. Okay?

IRISH MAN. I like to know where I stand.

JPW. Ten guineas a session – that's for six. But fifteen for the first in case it is going to be the only one. That was frankly put.

IRISH MAN. That's not too bad.

JPW. Do you think so?

IRISH MAN. It's fine.

JPW. Well, that was a good start. Well now, could we begin with your name?

IRISH MAN. Rather not.

JPW. That's good!

IRISH MAN. If you don't mind.

JPW. Your name! For God's sake, Mr – Mr, where has the orthodox route taken them? Into their very own not-very-pleasant strait-jackets. My style – as you have been observing – is casual.

IRISH MAN. I haven't much time for psychiatrists – psychologists.

JPW. Candid opinion? Intellectual philistines. Conflicting approaches, contradictory schools. And Freud! Now it transpires it was all about his having it off with his sister-in-law. Did you read about that? In the papers.

IRISH MAN. My wife wanted me to see a psychologist. Our doctor wanted me to see a psychiatrist, I told them the same thing.

JPW. What thing?

IRISH MAN. That I know more about life than the lot of them put together.

JPW. I see. So you chose me?

IRISH MAN *considering* JPW.

Actually this stubble is going to be a beard.

IRISH MAN. You're a stranger here, Mr King?

JPW. Well, I have been here for nearly – five years? I mean to say.

IRISH MAN. But you're a stranger, you're English?

JPW. Yes, yes, but a Tipperary grandmother. That's where I get it from. God rest her.

IRISH MAN. Public school?

JPW. Yes.

IRISH MAN. I'm a self-made man.

JPW. I gathered that – I mean, and aren't you proud of it!

IRISH MAN. But not university?

JPW. No, I broke my father's heart instead. But that's enough about me, what do you think of me? Joke. Yes, well, time to start getting down to those old levels of data. We have no

name, good. Address? No address, quite in order in my book.
Telephone — in case? No. Fine. Age?

IRISH MAN. Fifty-one.

JPW. Ah! That rules out a few things, what? Yes, well. Are
there many people of your acquaintance dying at the
moment?

IRISH MAN (*rising*). I think . . .

JPW. We're doing fine.

IRISH MAN. I think we may have made a mistake.

JPW	Absolutely fine! —
IRISH MAN	I'll maybe call some other time —
JPW	You came to consult me —
IRISH MAN	No, I —
JPW	For my help —
IRISH MAN	I don't know what I'm doing here —
JPW	That's what I'm here for! Please —

IRISH MAN. I don't need help! (*Hand in his pocket.*) I've got
the answer! Can't talk to anyone! I'm not insane!

JPW. I'm insane! There, you nearly laughed.

IRISH MAN. I didn't!

JPW. I am insane.

IRISH MAN. That's your problem.

JPW. I'm joking. That is what my father used to say, the boy is
a dreamer, he used to say, he's crazy. Strike root was his
phrase. Sit down, my friend. Mama, of course, was a different
kettle of fish: the inner world, and a little poetry. What was
your mother like?

IRISH MAN (*rounds on him*). Is it information you're looking
for?!

JPW. Or pace if you wish, yes, but, good heavens, if we cannot, two grown men, help one another. I mean to say do you think mental health means normal adjustment?

IRISH MAN. I don't want normal adjustment.

JPW. Exactly! Where is the achievement in standardised activity or routine trivia? Change your car, grow a carrot? I have to watch it myself, now that I have taken root. For God's sake, we might as well go back to Galileo Galilei, I say to my Helen.

IRISH MAN. I wouldn't call building more than a thousand houses routine trivia.

JPW. The house-proud life she would have me lead!

IRISH MAN. Apart from a thousand other deals.

JPW. So, you are a builder, a developer?

IRISH MAN. An 'operator'.

JPW. Got it. You have come to a standstill, you are looking for the will, the driveness to build a thousand more.

IRISH MAN. I don't want to build anything more. This – something – cloud has come down on me.

JPW. Has it happened before, is there a pattern?

IRISH MAN. I just felt I'd like an explanation.

JPW. Check. But no pattern?

IRISH MAN. I don't mind pain. I could always – still can – and I've a bad back – mix concrete shovel for shovel with any navvy if a machine broke down. But this other thing. I don't understand it.

JPW. No pattern. Anything else?

IRISH MAN. No.

JPW. When you were outside the door I thought you said –

IRISH MAN. No, nothing else! How much did you say? (*Preparing to go.*)

JPW. You just want an explanation –

IRISH MAN. Ten, fifteen pounds? –

JPW. You stated it as a fact.

IRISH MAN. There's too many facts in the world! Them houses were built out of facts: corruption, brutality, backhanding, fronthanding, backstabbing, lump labour and a bit of technology.

JPW. I should not have thought you the type.

IRISH MAN. Aaw! aren't yeh good? Oh, out there, boy, you learn how to take the main chance.

JPW. You don't have to pay me now. Your problem is –

IRISH MAN. Forget it. I have it here somewhere. Ten, eleven . . . fourteen . . .

JPW (*watching him make up the money with notes and coins*). . . . No, *you* forget it.

IRISH MAN (*sees JPW's offence; he laughs harshly*). My problem is. Yeh, I didn't think you were such a funny man when I saw you standing in the window. (*Puts money on desk.*) Fifteen pounds: fact.

JPW. Thank you. I owe you ten or fifteen minutes if you have no place else to go, and I do not think you have.

IRISH MAN. What would you like to talk about? You?

JPW. Anything you like.

IRISH MAN. D'yeh like me hat? . . . I've come to a standstill. I was never a great one to talk much. Now I'd prefer to walk a mile in the other direction than say how yeh or fuck yeh to anyone. In the mornings I say Christ how am I going to get through today. The house is silent though there's a child in it.

My wife is perplexed. She's so – good . . . D'yeh know what a slashhook is?

JPW. Like a sickle.

IRISH MAN. Yeh. With a long shaft and more lethal. Last night I decided I'd deal with the itinerants. I'd took a couple of sleeping pills, some wine, but I knew I was in for another night with my – music. (*Short, harsh laugh.*)

JPW. What pills?

IRISH MAN. Mandrax.

JPW. They've been taken off the market.

IRISH MAN (*ignores/dismisses this*). So, I decided I'd deal with the itinerants. The place is a shithouse, it's everywhere. Why did they choose me, my territory? And I know the doorsteps where it belongs. So. *Went* out. To kill them. But someone – the wife – called the police, and they stopped me. I would've killed them otherwise. No question about that. Jail – hospital mean nothing to me. Jail – hospital have a certain appeal. Then I listened to the record for the rest of the night.

JPW. The police?

IRISH MAN (*ignores/dismisses police*). This morning, then, the talks and whispers about psychiatrists – psychologists and their philosophy. (*Off, church clock chiming twelve.*) Time up?

JPW. No!

IRISH MAN. My – outbursts – are taking me by surprise. I don't know where the next one will lead me.

JPW. Yes! I mean to say, for a time, I started to play with the traffic. I mean, the startling thing, deliberately. Like a stiff-necked toreador in streets of highly dangerous traffic! I may have been a bull-fighter in a past life.

IRISH MAN. I want to sing.

JPW. That's one way of putting it.

IRISH MAN. I want to sing.

JPW. That's what I thought you said out there earlier.

IRISH MAN. Like Gigli. He was a tenor.

JPW. Why not Caruso?

IRISH MAN. It's Gigli.

JPW. Ah, we must not aim too high.

IRISH MAN (*sharply*). I've read one or two bits of snob things about Gigli.

JPW. Check. He was emotional, was he?

IRISH MAN. Caruso is another thing.

JPW. Check. You want to sing, like Gigli, inverted commas.

IRISH MAN. No inverted commas.

JPW. Cut inverted commas, how much do you drink?

IRISH MAN. You don't understand.

JPW. Oh, I understand –

IRISH MAN. Drink is not a problem for me!

JPW. Exactly! Increase in alcohol tolerance. Excuse me! Inability to discuss problem, grandiose statements and aggressive behaviour – memory blackouts? – unreasonable resentments, physical deterioration – loss of weight? – vague spiritual desires – nearly finished – inability to initiate action – Enough? Alibis exhausted, defeat admitted? Desire for recovery – How much do you drink?

IRISH MAN. I'm – a – very – poor – drinker, Mr King.

JPW. Wine and those sleeping pills, lethal. People in America jumping out of windows on wings of Mandrax.

IRISH MAN *opens his mouth.*

I'm sorry – I enjoy a challenge, and this is a challenging one, but – But! – if we are to get to our objective, to sing, we have enough layers to destratify without being hampered by toxic liquids, so all drink out! – Give it a try? – Good man. Now, tell me everything . . . Except your name.

IRISH MAN *toys with his hat for a moment.*

Yes, it becomes you. Place, time, date of birth is always a good starting point.

IRISH MAN. I was born with a voice and little else.

JPW. Naked we came into the world.

IRISH MAN. We were very poor.

JPW. What did your father do?

IRISH MAN. A cobbler.

JPW. Making or mending them? It could be significant.

IRISH MAN. He started by making them but factory-made shoes soon put paid to that.

JPW. Where was this?

IRISH MAN. Recanati.

JPW. Recan?

IRISH MAN. Ati.

JPW. What county is that in?

IRISH MAN. Recanati is in Italy.

JPW. Italian born?

IRISH MAN. My hair was a lot darker some years ago. Sing us a song-a, Benimillo, the people used to say. I knew all the pop songs and, as you know, all the famous arias are part of our – our culture.

JPW. Got your first name.

IRISH MAN. It was a pet name.

JPW. Benimillo.

IRISH MAN. I wasn't a great boy soprano but I was the best around. I read, the really good boy sopranos tend to develop later as bassos or baritones, so not being that alto – although good – I had it there as well.

JPW. As an indication that your future was to be a tenor. The clouds are beginning to clear at last, Benimillo. (*He finishes the vodka in the bottle behind* IRISH MAN's *back.*)

IRISH MAN. I sang in the choir, of course. And we sang, oh, Gregorian Chant and, oh, all sorts of things like the sacred music of Rossini and Gounod.

JPW. 'Thieving Magpie' – What time is it?

IRISH MAN. Quarter past twelve.

JPW. Good! Well, let's see what we have now.

IRISH MAN. And then, one day, these three young men come all the way from Macerata, and all because of me.

JPW. What did they want?

IRISH MAN. They wanted me to dress up as a girl and sing the soprano role in an operetta, 'Angelica's Elopement'.

JPW. Strangers?

IRISH MAN. No. But such a thing was out of the question, my mother said.

JPW. I should think so.

IRISH MAN. No. But she said she was sorry they'd made such a long journey for nothing but 'twas their own fault and then she sent them packing.

JPW. Good! Well let's see what we have now.

IRISH MAN. But they weren't to be put off that easy.

JPW. They came back.

IRISH MAN. They came back, pleading. They said I'd have a share of the profits. Well, my father said – he was still alive at the time. After all, he said, there's no great harm in it. Not that my mother ever paid much heed to him. She always looked to Abramo, me eldest brother. Abramo was the real figure of authority in our house.

JPW. What did Abramo say?

IRISH MAN. Well, my mother got a little surprise because, after thinking, Abramo said that he personally couldn't see anything in it to frown about. (*A smile of minor triumph.*) Hah?

JPW. Very interesting, truly, Benimillo, but I think I have now got sufficient data on –

IRISH MAN. No –

JPW. For instance, I played Yum-Yum, 'The Mikado' you know? at boarding school and came out of the experience comparatively unscathed.

IRISH MAN. The next few weeks were fraught, fraught with excitement. Trips to Macerata, rehearsals, and we played, not in a grimy little hall, but in the municipal theatre. Someone had to push me on the stage. Then, suddenly, everything was all right and I sauntered back and forth with me parasol singing 'Passigiando un anno fa'. I couldn't hardly believe my ears that all the cries of 'Bis! Bis!' was really for me.

JPW. Bis.

IRISH MAN. To tell the God's honest truth, I felt ashamed like, getting so much more of the clapping than the others.

JPW. *Your accent* – you must have been very young when you came to this country?

IRISH MAN. But I'd filled the hall with my voice, held the crowd. They understood. And, I thought, I can do it again. I will do it again.

JPW. But it was on to the building trade.

IRISH MAN. I suppose the experience made me – giddy. But I don't know. 'Twas more than that. And 'twasn't the clapping. Like, you can talk forever, but singing. Singing, d'yeh know? The only possible way to tell people.

JPW. What?

IRISH MAN (*shrugs, he does not know*). . . . Who you are? . . . But Abramo said, you may have been to . . . to . . . to . . .

JPW. Macerata?

IRISH MAN. Macerata, singing and play-acting, but that doesn't mean you forget your manners or the straits this family is in, or the job I had to look after.

JPW. In the building trade?

IRISH MAN (*ire rising*). In the – what? – No! – The shop – messenger-boy – the local pharmacia, whatever the ('*Fuck that is.*') – A shop-boy, messenger-boy, dogsbody – my brother was a tyrant!

JPW. Good! Well, let us see now –

IRISH MAN (*harsh, intense*). And the man I worked for, *he* was an alcoholic, a quack, a parasite, a failure in everything, ate rat poison one night and I came to this country shortly after!

JPW. . . . I mean, that it is time, and I wanted to sum up.

IRISH MAN. Sum up *what*?

JPW. Your depression – that you are undergoing severe –

IRISH MAN. What does that mean (*Depression.*): Everything mean and low?!

JPW. Dispirited, humbled, yes, brought low.

IRISH MAN. Everything mean and low?!

JPW. Reduction in pitch of voice?

IRISH MAN. Do you mean I'm unhappy?

JPW. I should imagine so.

IRISH MAN. Then I'm unhappy!

JPW. That's good: anger, let it all come out. That is what I shall be aiming at.

IRISH MAN. What have you been writing there?

JPW. Confidential –

IRISH MAN. What have you been writing down? –

JPW. Your file. Unethical –

IRISH MAN *snaps the sheet of paper from* JPW.

A matter between your GP and myself.

IRISH MAN (*reading*). 'Facts. There are too many facts in the world.'

JPW. Interesting observation of yours.

IRISH MAN. 'Fiction. Fantasy' (*He looks at* JPW *who averts his eyes.*) . . . 'Bis'.

JPW. Encore?

IRISH MAN. 'Towards the end of the session he smiled.'

JPW. You did, we made progress.

IRISH MAN. 'Pot of jam, tea, saccharin.'

JPW. I do not take sugar. You might not think it, but I am still vain.

IRISH MAN. Do you think I'm a fool?

JPW. No. And I am not one either.

IRISH MAN. You were summing up.

JPW. That you are deeply unhappy – presently –

IRISH MAN. Aren't you?

JPW. And psychotic.

IRISH MAN. Me?

JPW. Yes.

IRISH MAN. What's psychotic?

JPW. Out of control.

IRISH MAN. Is that so? (*Face contorted in impotent hatred.*) Anything else?

JPW. You do not like what you are.

IRISH MAN. Better than not knowing *who* or what I am!

JPW. Another appointment in town, actually running late, but let me see, yes, I can manage, fortunately, another session tomorrow, same time – well, perhaps a little later. Twelve o'clock?

IRISH MAN. I don't think so. (*Going out.*)

JPW. I can make you sing! And remember –

IRISH MAN *is gone.*

. . . all drink out. (*He polishes off the remainder of his vodka.*) He's crazy.

He sticks a book in his pocket, is collecting up the money.
MONA *is entering with some fruit and cigarettes for him.*

MONA. Well, lover! Who was that I met on the stairs? (*She opens out the couch.*) How about a session?

He is already gone out the door. She puts down the fruit and the cigarettes.

No joy here, productive or otherwise! Here, there, elsewhere, where? Perhaps tonight. (*She crouches down as if talking to a child.*) So, little one, shall we go look at the sea? Too boring, cold, polluted? Bewley's then, again: tea and cakes. Or, the ezzo? (*Zoo.*) cinema? to see more shite. Ahm ah, we'll ah . . . be talking about it on the way home. Aa, fuck it, child, let's go somewhere.

She is leaving. Lights fading, up sound: Gigli singing 'O Paradiso'.

Scene Two

Off, church clock chiming twelve. JPW huddled in bed in a drunken stupor, asleep. Bell on outer door ringing, silhouette of IRISH MAN coming to office door, knocking . . .

IRISH MAN. Mr King! . . . Mr King! . . .

Silhouette pacing to and fro for a few moments, then leaving. Lights fading, up sound: Gigli continuing 'O Paradiso'.

Scene Three

JPW on phone.

JPW. Same answer I suppose. (*He nods gravely to her reply. Then:*) 'Bye . . . What? . . . Oh, couple of interviews in town and . . . Oh, what am I doing now, at this very moment? Stack of letters in front of me requiring attention and, you know, very busy . . . No, I'm still here . . . What? . . . I try . . . I promise . . . 'Bye. (*He puts the phone down.*) 'Please, please, don't phone me again.' I try. Helen.

He goes to the window and lets up the blind. Then reacting to someone watching his window from the street and into action: phone apparatus readjusted, bed reconverted, spectacles for effect, etc. He unlocks the door, opens it, sits on the couch with a book, as if reading it. Church clock chiming two. IRISH MAN has arrived. He stands in the doorway abjectly.

This is a fine time of day! Come in.

IRISH MAN *continues, abject, in the doorway.*

But when I say twelve o'clock I mean twelve o'clock! Come in! (*He looks at IRISH MAN for the first time and becomes unnerved.*) And how was your evening? Jolly? On the town?

A night at the opera? . . . Yes, well, but, to sing like Gigli in six easy lessons!

IRISH MAN (*continues in doorway*). Are you married?

JPW. . . . Am I?

IRISH MAN. A saint is she.

JPW. A saint is she yes, I must admit she is pretty special. Irish colleen, apron, you know? darns my socks, that kind of thing.

IRISH MAN. Children.

JPW. Two.

IRISH MAN (*quietly*). I built a fire at home last night and burned all the toys in the house. What am I to do?

JPW. You may smoke if you wish.

IRISH MAN. Everything so stale, so mean and low. Stupid, numbed, guilty, worthless, finished . . . Finished? Naaw! (*Coming into the room.*) Do you live here, Mr King?

JPW. No.

IRISH MAN. I envy it.

JPW. I don't.

IRISH MAN. Then where do you live?

JPW. Nothing very large, of course, but clematis round the door, that sort of dwelling. Perhaps in one of your own sylvan developments?

IRISH MAN. With the wife?

JPW. She does not have to darn my socks, of course, but that is her nature. Even when they have got no holes in them? (*He laughs. Silence. He sits.*) There's nothing staler than death, my friend.

IRISH MAN (*suddenly wild*). And what about me?

JPW *uncomprehending.*

I! Me! I! What I want!

JPW. And that is why we are here.

IRISH MAN. What *I* feel!

JPW. Check.

IRISH MAN. Inside!

JPW. Yes! Gigli!

IRISH MAN. He's the devil!

JPW. He's the? Oh for God's sake, Benimillo, snap out of it.

IRISH MAN. That's a – a stupid – ridiculous thing to say!
   D'yeh think I'd be this way if I could help it? When I listen to
   him – I-can't-stop-listening-to-him! Fills me! The – things –
   inside. Tense, everything more intense. And I listen carefully.
   And it's beautiful – But it's screaming, it's longing! Longing
   for what? I don't know whether it's keeping me sane or
   driving me crazy. You may laugh.

JPW. I am not laughing.

IRISH MAN. Or is it mocking me?

JPW. Music hath charms to –

IRISH MAN. Naaw, whoever said that is a fool. A record! A
   Christmas present! Or what does it want me to do? Fly!

JPW. Stop listening to him.

IRISH MAN. I'll see it through. My wife is near nervous
   breakdown. She's barely holding on. She says I look like an
   old man. Hah?

JPW. And so you do.

IRISH MAN. She looks like an old woman. She was a princess.
   You should have seen her. Even three months ago. She's
   holding on for me she says, not the child. The child too, but

why on earth for me? And I burned all his toys last night. I rooted them out of every corner. And I'm so proud of him. I see him watching me sometimes. He's almost nine. I watch him sometimes too, secretly, and wonder will I write him a letter. Or take him for a little walk, my arm around his shoulders. Because, though he's nearly nine, and a boy, he would still allow me put my arm around his shoulders. My son. And explain to him that I don't matter. That it would be better if I disappeared.

JPW. Ah, Mr . . .

IRISH MAN. And sometimes I wish things on them ('*Dead*.') that I don't want to wish them, things that are maybe going to turn out unlucky.

JPW. Ah, Mr . . .

IRISH MAN. My wife come down last night. Nightdress, long hair. I pretended I didn't hear her come in or that she was watching me. And I kept listening to the music. Then she come and stood beside my chair. Smiling. What are you listening to. I use the headphones at night. Elgar, I said. I don't know why I said that because the only thing I listen to is him. And. You off I said. To bed. And she said yes, it's ten past one heighho. And. You coming up she said. And I said, in a little, I said. And. Then she knelt down and put her head on my knees. And then she said talk to me. Talk to me, talk to me, please love talk to me. And I couldn't think of a single thing to say. And then she said I love you so much. And I said I love you too . . . but not out loud. And. Then she got up. And then she said pull yourself together, what's the matter with you, for God's sake get a grip on yourself, pull yourself together. She was trembling. She'd let go for a moment. And then she said goodnight. When she left I stood up. Out of respect. I knew she would've stopped in the hall. She usually does. Just stands there for a few moments. Before going up. And. Then it came out. My roar. Fuck you, fuck you . . . fuck you. (*Though delivered quietly and the intense emotion contained, tears have started down the* IRISH MAN's *face during the speech.*)

JPW. Ah, Mr . . . I'm out of my depth. This organisation, Steve, our founder, leader, came over and set up this office. Though I have always wanted to achieve something, I couldn't do even that much on my own. They sent me over here. But even they have forgotten me. And I have forgotten them. I think it is likely they shipped Steve back to the States. I do not even know if we are still in existence.

IRISH MAN. Then-why-do-you-stay-on-in-this-terrible-country-then!

JPW (*a gesture to the window, 'Helen', changes his mind, and follows with the peculiarly defensive reply under the circumstances*). That's – that is my affair! I'm out of my depth.

IRISH MAN ⎤ No, you're not –
JPW   ⎟ I'm out of my depth!
IRISH MAN ⎟ No, you're not.
JPW   ⎬ I have no answers, I'm at my wit's end –
IRISH MAN ⎟ No, you're not, no you're not –
JPW   ⎦ Good grief, trying to work things out, all my life, for myself.

IRISH MAN. Your Helen, your dwelling, your –

JPW. Yes, my – That is none of your business!

IRISH MAN. I'm happy with you.

JPW. There is no organisation! –

IRISH MAN. I'm happy with you, Mr King –

JPW. A real, recognised, qualified, university-trained psychiatrist you need.

IRISH MAN *rolling his head.*

What have you against them?

IRISH MAN. They don't know! Philosophy! And people like
them – I've dealt with them – I've had them on the building
sites – walking fast in pinstripe suits – that's all they know –
or fucked-up by too much education – that's all they know!

JPW. They can see patterns.

IRISH MAN. I'm happy with you.

JPW	('*No.*') I don't mind making a fast buck –
IRISH MAN	I have a lot of time for instinct –
JPW	I don't mind telling you I need the shillings –
IRISH MAN	Always used instinct –
JPW	But, in fairness, I draw the line. I am not, though you might think it, a ponce.

IRISH MAN. Instinct, my strength, boy. Unerring instinct for
the right man for the job.

JPW. This is not a job!

IRISH MAN. I'll get to the root of this, I'll see it through, my
way. I've never been beaten – Oh, they tried, but I left a few
cripples around the place. I've taken on, done business with
the big – (*Whispers.*) the biggest in the land – and there was
nothing he, or they, could teach little me. Never been beaten,
a survivor, and this isn't going to beat me either.

JPW. Gently for a second. For what it is worth, my opinion: in
any game it is dangerous taking up arms against an unknown
enemy.

IRISH MAN (*hand in pocket*). And if all comes to all, I have
the trump card.

JPW. Gently, for a second. Are we talking about singing? I
mean, can you be serious?

IRISH MAN. Oh, I'm always serious –

JPW. To *sing*? –

IRISH MAN. I could never afford to be anything but serious!

JPW. Benimillo –

IRISH MAN. I'm so serious –

JPW. Benimillo! –

IRISH MAN. You look out – you-look-out! – cause I'm going to get you too!

JPW (*silently*). Well-well!

IRISH MAN. So is my time up for today?

JPW. I should imagine it is. I have some meditating to do.

IRISH MAN. So what time tomorrow?

JPW. Tomorrow is Saturday, I do not work weekends.

IRISH MAN. I'll pay you in advance? – For the remaining four sessions. Cash or – it'll have to be a cheque.

JPW. And you want a session on Sunday? Well-well! That was not a very kind thing to say to a friend, Benimillo.

IRISH MAN. How much?

JPW. Double-time for Saturday and Sunday.

IRISH MAN. A hundred pounds.

JPW. Gosh! A hundred pounds. Your desperation is fantastic. A hundred is fine and a cheque is fine and the banks are still open.

IRISH MAN. What time tomorrow?

JPW. Your choice.

IRISH MAN. You'll be here?

JPW. State the time.

IRISH MAN. You'll be here?

JPW. I'll be here.

IRISH MAN (*about to hand over the cheque, remembers*). I'll be back with cash in two minutes.

IRISH MAN *goes out.*

JPW. Nearly got your second name, *Benimillo!* . . . Jesus Christ!

JPW *reflective, then an idea; telephone directory, finds a number, adjustment to telephone apparatus* . . .

Hospitals, hospitals. What am I doing? – He's crazy! St Anne's, administration, nurses' residence, X-ray department. No. St Godolph's, unusual one, administration, nurses' – ah! (*Raps out a number.*) Psychiatric department, please . . . Good afternoon. The psychiatrist in charge, please . . . his assistant then . . . any psychiatrist . . . yes, an appointment . . . no, for my brother . . . for today . . . next month! . . . Couldn't she see me tomorrow? . . . I know tomorrow is Saturday, Miss, but I have got my brother outside, now, literally tied up with ropes in the boot of the car . . . Miss, I'm a practising GP and this is not a case for your casualty department . . . Madam, I am sitting on a barrel of gun powder, can-you-help-me? . . . Monday. What time? . . . That's very early . . . I said that is fine . . . What? . . . Oh, Mickeleen O'Loughlin. (*He puts phone down.*)

IRISH MAN *returns and slaps the money on the desk.*

IRISH MAN. Noon tomorrow! And you had better be here! Do you understand that?

JPW *striking head to head pose with* IRISH MAN *across the desk.*

JPW. You bring the pistols! I shall bring the booze!

Up music, final section of 'O Paradiso', to conclude the scene.

Scene Four

JPW *and* MONA *in bed, swapping a bottle of vodka.* JPW *drinking hard to fortify himself. On the floor beside the bed some books, charts; some groceries on the desk.*

MONA *is thirty-eight. Her moods can alternate as quickly as her thoughts, but her vitality, generosity and seemingly celebratory nature allow her to hold a 'down' mood only fleetingly. She is dressed in a white slip.*

MONA. You're not listening to me.

He nods.

I shouldn't have dropped in?

He nods.

You're bored now?

He nods. She kicks him or whatever.

So I dashed out to take my god-child to her ballet class. Dashed back home. Pacing the floor: what to do now? *And-I-was ravenous* – for something. So I ate three eggs, then two yoghurts: still wondering, what'll I do now? So I thought I'll chance you.

JPW. Well, I am going to see this thing through too.

MONA. You're not listening to me!

JPW. He may even shoot me if I don't.

MONA. Who?

JPW. Benimillo the Irish man. A practical man, like my father. But this practical man is declaring that the romantic kingdom *is* of this world.

MONA. And that's all you were doing last night, reading?

JPW. I *want* him to prove it. I am contracted to assist him.

MONA. If I had known. (*Head under the bedclothes.*) Freezing in here.

JPW. Do you see what I mean? And I have been up all night. And I had it all figured out at one point. I got very excited. Now I've forgotten it all.

MONA (*under the bedclothes*). Nothing much happening down here, my friend.

JPW. Pardon? No! No! You should not be doing this to me.

MONA. Seducing you, lover?

JPW. Yes, and bringing those – groceries! – over here. What on earth am I to do when he arrives? I must keep it on a conversational level at all costs. But how does one do that?

MONA. Keep on talking.

JPW. Pardon?

MONA. You keep on talking.

JPW. Yes! Because, I mean to say, I am not *that* afraid of him.

MONA. And shock them if you can.

JPW. Yes, I'm sure he's a Catholic.

   She laughs.

   Are you a Catholic?

MONA (*nods*). And I pray.

JPW. What is original sin?

MONA. Screw original sin.

JPW. Existential guilt.

MONA. What about my problems?!

JPW. What problems?

MONA. I'm a subject.

JPW. You jump into bed as soon as you come in that door.

MONA. That's my problem.

JPW. I was lucky to escape the other day.

MONA. That's why I came early this morning. (*She gets up, starts to dress.*)

JPW. What are you doing?

MONA. Another port of call.

JPW. Where to?

MONA. Oh? A man. Does funny things to me. Are you jealous? You: fat chance.

JPW. Don't go yet.

MONA. All right. My chin is as sore, is it all red? What'll my husband say? I'm annoyed now I didn't think of batteries for your shaver.

JPW (*absently*). Did you think of a pot of jam?

MONA (*solemn nod 'Yes' and followed by a solemn tone as she gets back into bed*). But I have to collect my god-child. Then to the doctor.

JPW. What-is-life?

MONA. Life, my friend, is bouncing back. But, I suppose I was lucky to get in here at all, hmm? The bars are going up around town against old Mona. And some – curtain – is being drawn. Jimmy. Promise me something. That you'll let me down gently.

JPW. What are you talking about?

MONA. Now that you ask. I'm not quite sure. Or where I am or what I'm at. I know there's someone else but I'm not too bad, am I?

JPW (*defensively*). What someone else?

MONA. But I *know* it! Look at you now: eyes like a wounded – nun.

JPW. I'm forty-six.

MONA. Who is she? – just for interest's sake.

JPW. I'm very flattered.

MONA. I'm twenty-eight. Okay, thirty-eight. And nothing to show for it yet. When I get into bed with you I say right, Mona, down to work, fifteen times today.

JPW. We did it twice the time before last.

MONA. *My* doing. And you're only a baby – all men are babies – and I'd hate to have big tits.

JPW. I never said –

MONA. Some men do! (*Then she laughs.*) In the past. Well, what is it about me, tell me? – as against Miss-whoever-she-is. And she doesn't look after you very well, does she? (*She indicates the room.*)

JPW. You are a respectable married woman!

Then they laugh. Then she becomes grave.

MONA. Don't laugh at me. You don't know what it's like. 'Good old Mona.' *And*, I don't like being used.

JPW. Yes, well, but, Mona, I sometimes feel –

MONA. That's the first time you used my named today.

JPW. Yes, but, well, I sometimes feel that you are possibly, I mean to say, using me. (*She nods gravely.*) I mean, the interesting thing, who picked up whom that evening in the supermarket?

MONA. At the health-food counter.

JPW. I have often wondered.

MONA. My magician. (*Impulsively.*) I'll give you the money to have that phone reconnected.

JPW. I'm a wage-earner now, I have a job.

MONA. Suit yourself.

JPW. . . . What's wrong with Karen, this famous god-child of yours?

MONA (*insists*). Karen-Marie. (*Maree.*)

JPW. Karen-Marie.

MONA. I'm going to the doctor.

JPW. What's wrong with you?

MONA. I fancy the doctor.

JPW. I wouldn't put it past you.

MONA. Where would you put it? . . . You don't like those remarks.

He gets it and laughs.

But, at least you deign to talk to me when I'm here. Not like some. And not like that string of misery I have at home. (*She grunts in imitation of her husband.*) I'm leaving him. Don't worry, not because of you. And I have him worn out too. (*Sighs.*) I should have married a farmer.

JPW. Six children.

MONA. Double it. Now you're getting close. Here, I'll give you a laugh. You know how I take that god-child everywhere with me? But-can-I-stop-her-dawdling-behind! We were shopping during the week and we had to go through the men's wear department to get to the ladies' wear and suddenly this voice, 'Madam! Madam!' This poor shop-assistant, eighty, if he was a day. And I looked around for Karen-Marie. And you know shop-dummies? Well, there she was, innocent as you like, looking up at their faces, unzipping their flies and putting her hand inside. 'Madam! Madam!' And I'm shouting . . . There's someone outside.

Silhouette of IRISH MAN *arriving outside, tapping the door.*

Is that him?

JPW. Stay where you are.

MONA. Ah, Jimmy –

JPW. I shan't be long, Benimillo! (*Silhouette moving away.*) No, let him wait – bloody hell – he's early. What am I going to say to him? Unzipping their flies, putting her hand inside, putting her hand inside. (*He is in a panic, whispering: does not know what he's saying.*)

MONA (*continues in a whisper, dressing hurriedly*). 'Madam! Madam!' And I'm shouting 'Karen-Marie! Karen-Marie!' 'Madam! Madam!' 'Karen-Marie! Karen-Marie!' And says Karen-Marie – (*To* JPW.) Don't be looking at me (*Dressing.*) – 'They're only dummies', she said, 'they have no willies'. Well laugh!

JPW. Well laugh, they have no willies. (*Putting on his trousers, etc.*)

MONA. And the other women about were in hysterics.

JPW. Hystrics and what happened then?

MONA. And what happened then . . . (*She appears peculiarly lost for a moment.*) I think I'm going crazy. Am I forgetting anything?

Off, church clock chiming twelve.

Jesus! – Twelve o'clock! – How do I get out of here?

JPW. He's not my wife.

MONA. You haven't got a wife. (*Adjusting her bodice, referring to her breasts.*) If it fits in your mouth it's big enough. See yeh – will I? – get the phone mended will yeh, see yeh.

He lets her out and shuts the door. He is smoking, drinking, leaves the bed uncovered – trying to assert a defiance – opens the door on the last chime of the church clock, strikes a pose with a chart or book, his back to the door, and waits.

IRISH MAN *comes to stand in the doorway, smiling; he is carrying a large cardboard box. He looks pleased with himself this morning.*

IRISH MAN. Can I come in? I arrived a bit early I'm afraid. Can I come in?

JPW. Come in.

IRISH MAN. I did a little shopping. I brought the pistols. Can I put it here? . . . Hah? . . . Hah? . . . It's easy enough put together . . . Hah?

IRISH MAN *chuckling 'Hah', producing a new record-player from the box, and a record.*

JPW *is thrown, surprised and resentful of this move, but trying to contain himself.*

JPW. You mean to say you bought that?

IRISH MAN. Hah? The wife? (*Mona.*)

JPW. No, not the wife, Benimillo. Drink? While I am *waiting* for you.

IRISH MAN. Thanks, yes, why not, please.

JPW. Oh?

IRISH MAN. Weekend. She was wearing a ring.

JPW. She wasn't! Begod! Another man's wife, Benimillo, are you shocked?

IRISH MAN. Good luck!

JPW. She's a Catholic.

IRISH MAN. And what does your own wife think about all this in your sylvan dwelling?

JPW *reacts angrily, sweeping the groceries off the desk into drawers or wherever.*

. . . I didn't mean to offend you or . . . Wha'?

JPW. Ah, sure man dear alive, a mac, sure I know well you didn't sure! And that machine set you back a few quid, five or six hundred?

IRISH MAN. Are you having an affair, Mr King?

JPW. She may think so.

IRISH MAN. Oh now, that's a bit chauvinist.

JPW ('*Gosh! Chauvinist!*') What did you think of her?

IRISH MAN. A fine woman.

JPW. But her tits – you don't fancy big tits then?

IRISH MAN. Is there a power-point somewhere?

JPW. I knew this Irish chap once had a big thing about (*Mimes.*) round electric light switches.

IRISH MAN (*finds the power-point*). Here we are.

JPW. Ah but sure if it fits in your mouth it's big enough.

IRISH MAN. Anything more is a waste. (*In reaction to* JPW's *surprise.*) That's what we used to say all right. If it fits in your mouth it's big enough, anything more is a waste.

JPW. But, but – personally, Benimillo – big or small, they are startling things, and I am always astonished at how casually the ladies themselves take them for granted.

IRISH MAN. There we are. (*Set up.*)

JPW. Would you agree with that observation?

IRISH MAN (*switches on machine – orchestral opening bars of 'O Paradiso'*). D'yeh mind?

JPW. I do.

IRISH MAN (*cueing to another track*). No, not this first one, it starts with 'O Paradiso' but there's a piece here –

JPW. I said I do mind!

IRISH MAN. Wha'?

JPW. I said no! (*He switches off the machine.*)

IRISH MAN. I just want you to listen to him.

JPW. You want to listen to him or you want to sing like him,
which? Sit down. We have work to do. Look at this chart,
please. (*He holds up a chart or he draws a chart – three
circles, connecting lines, etc. – on the wall.*)

IRISH MAN (*placatory*). I enjoy our meetings, Mr King.

JPW. You see this circle here, the most perfect of shapes, the
cosmic womb, the clear pool of being. We travel down this
line –

IRISH MAN. I look forward to them.

JPW. We-travel-down-this-line to our second pool, existence,
the here and now. Again the most perfect of shapes, but look
at what is inside: a mess.

IRISH MAN. I enjoy them –

JPW. Circles within circles, concentric and eccentric, squiggles,
swirls of objects, and at the bottom, this dark area here,
sediment: despair. Our problem, to achieve the state of clear
which exists here, in our second pool, here. But,
paradoxically, it is from this dark area, this rising darkness of
our despair that the solution is to derive, if – if! – we can get
it to rise to cover the whole pool and blot out our squiggles
and circles and what-nots. Good.

IRISH MAN. What's the third pool?

JPW. Indeed. And I should be grateful if you did not interrupt
me further. The areas we shall be going into from here on in
are not without risk, and will demand not only your
concentration, but that courage required for an encounter of
a most strange and singular kind.

IRISH MAN. You're having me on. (*Smiling, uneasy with this
kind of talk.*)

JPW. Pardon?

IRISH MAN. Aw!

JPW. 'Aw'?

IRISH MAN. Naaw!

JPW. 'Naaw'? You are not saying, I hope, that you thought the simple problem you have set us would be solved in the traditional way? I mean by sitting down together and playing that game called Slobs. The winner proves himself to be the most sentimental player and becomes King Slob by dealing, at the most unexpected moment, an emotional kick in the genitals to his opponent, thereby *getting* him. Problem solved.

IRISH MAN. I was out of sorts yesterday.

JPW. But we had a good night last night, had we, slept well?

IRISH MAN. No.

JPW. The three aspects which we shall concentrate on today are, one, your existential guilt, two, its twin paralysing demon, the I-am-who-am syndrome, and three, despair. Then, if you are up to it, we shall over the next three days set to possibilising that quiet power of the possible waiting within you.

IRISH MAN. Naaw, aw!

JPW. 'Naaw – aw' *again*! Explain yourself. Ah! You are impatient to ask what is your natural existential guilt.

IRISH MAN. Guilt – exist – I'm not guilty of anything.

JPW	Heard you yesterday, imprisoned, numbed, guilty.
IRISH MAN	Survival! – What am I guilty of, survival? D'yeh know what's going on out there?
JPW	The point is you feel guilty.
IRISH MAN	And innocent at the same time!

JPW. That's good! Just like Adam when he got the boot.

IRISH MAN. *Adam?*

JPW. What have I done he said to God, I only – But God said, out, out!

IRISH MAN. I don't know what you're talking about.

JPW. But what had Adam done? No, it was not a deed. It was much later that the screwing started. Adam did not lose his head over Eve in the Garden, he lost his tail – when he bit the apple. He *gained* a head, knowledge – Tree of Knowledge – a little of which, one bite, is a dangerous thing. He started thinking – *thinking* – and self-consciousness crept in, which is existential guilt, which is original sin.

IRISH MAN. What's this got to do with it?

JPW. Out of the Garden, on to clearing the jungle, developing it, mind-numbing drudgery to stop the pain of what they had lost. On to milking the goats, cutting the grass, trying to get Cain to toe a more conservative and respectable line, standardised activity, routine trivia, looking for the new security.

IRISH MAN. *You* don't know what you're talking about!

JPW (*confronting* IRISH MAN). And all the time obliterating the side of their nautre that was innocent and beautiful, as if it were the side that is vulgar, vicious, mean, ruthless, offensive, dangerous, obscene! What are you doing? What are you – ?

IRISH MAN *has gone to record-player and cued in a track. He faces* JPW *squarely, a dangerous and warning attitude, telling* JPW *not to interfere. Gigli singing 'Dai campi, dai prati'. They listen to the aria.* JPW *conceals his appreciation of the singing.* IRISH MAN *switches off the machine and waits with a childlike expectation for an appreciative reaction.*

IRISH MAN. That's not my favourite, but because of that I thought you might like it best. What did you think of him?

JPW. Sobs a bit much, doesn't he, pouts a bit much?

IRISH MAN. That's the snobbery I was talking about!

JPW. And those 'h' sounds.

IRISH MAN. King!

JPW (*has picked up the record sleeve*). Yes, '*Beniamino*'.

IRISH MAN (*muttering furiously*). Oh but the English, the English, what would they know anyway!

JPW. Do you know what he was singing?

IRISH MAN. You don't have to! –

JPW. Did you understand the words? –

IRISH MAN. You don't –

JPW. What opera was that piece from? –

IRISH MAN. You don't have to know! I could always size a man up more from the sound he makes than from what he's saying.

JPW. Your unerring instinct. (*Looking at record sleeve.*) '*Mefistofele*': ah yes, he *is* the devil.

IRISH MAN. We were making little gold crosses over here when ye, over there, were still living in holes in the ground.

JPW. I do not doubt your word on it but what precisely is your point?

IRISH MAN. Oh, but very cold people the English, the British – Oh! and your Empire: that's located somewhere now in – what's them little islands called?

JPW. Oh, come, you can do better than that, you who have dealt and fenced and parried with the highest in the land. Have another drink, it will stimulate you. Here.

IRISH MAN *sends a chair careering across the room with a kick; he is about to smash his glass, and possibly JPW as well.*

IRISH MAN. Do you know who you're dealing with?

JPW. Be my guest (*Smash the glass.*) . . . I find I am not afraid of you. Despite the path you have left behind you strewn with cripples – and corpses? Jail, hospital, or – (*Mimes shooting himself in the head.*) mean nothing to me either. But I have only two glasses remaining in the house and if you smash that one, I shall certainly break this precious bottle over your head before you make a second move.

IRISH MAN (*a warning*). Don't try to take him (*Gigli.*) away from me, Mr King.

JPW. On the contrary. I am beginning to find this project most exciting. I intend to see it through. You say similarly, but I have an instinct too, and something is bothering me about *your* commitment. (*He pours drinks.*)

IRISH MAN. To sing!

JPW. That's good! Repeat it.

IRISH MAN. To sing, to sing! (*And drinks.*)

JPW. And I want you to go on repeating it. Yes, cheers! Because the most dangerous approach to our work from here-on-in is the half-longing half-frightened one. Look at our chart, please – the third pool, the one you asked about. One false step and not only do you miss your target but you end up out here, pool three, questionmark pool, banana-land!

IRISH MAN (*helping himself to another drink*). You'd know about it out there!

JPW. I am simply obliged to warn you.

IRISH MAN. Cheers-cheers-cheers!

JPW. And you may never come back. (*Laughing, getting carried away with himself.*) You may never come back to the poxy, boring anchor of this everyday world you have sold your soul for!

IRISH MAN. What of it?

JPW. The poxy boring anchor of this everyday world that others of us are shut out from!

IRISH MAN. What of it!

JPW. Indeed! The choice is yours! But I must be convinced of your commitment, and –

IRISH MAN. Wait a minute –

JPW. You are the one, to my mind, beginning to falter.

IRISH MAN. Wait a minute, what did you say?

JPW. What did I say?

IRISH MAN. There's something all along not making sense.

JPW. Well, of course, I have not as yet explained the paralysing I-am-who-am syndrome.

IRISH MAN. No. The poxy everyday world that others of us are shut out from? . . . This house of yours, sylvan dwelling – this wife of yours?

JPW. Allow me to complete my thesis, please.

IRISH MAN. Them groceries, two glasses in the house – this wife of yours?

JPW. Questions, if you have any, on the foregoing, please –

IRISH MAN. You have a very strange life of it here, Mr King –

JPW. Otherwise, please allow me to continue.

IRISH MAN. Are you separated, Mr King? Divorced?

JPW. Well, there goes our session.

IRISH MAN. Hmm?

JPW. Thank you, that will be all for today. (*He has opened the door.*)

IRISH MAN. No.

JPW. Yes! I am conducting things here.

IRISH MAN (*smiling, assessing*). Hmm? (*Then he laughs.*)

JPW (*bluffing*). Or – and I am loath to suggest it – you would rather perhaps we discontinued the whole thing entirely?

IRISH MAN. No –

JPW. Yes! – and had a refund of your money? . . . Yes?

IRISH MAN (*considers, then calls* JPW's *bluff*). Yes.

JPW. . . . Well, a refund is not going to be entirely possible. (*Offers what money he has.*) Your name will be included in the draw next week for the rest of it.

IRISH MAN (*refusing money*). Not interested in the money . . . So what do we do? Well. (*Going to the door. Bluffing about leaving.*) Do we continue tomorrow? It's up to you.

JPW. You don't have to go right now. Do you? I mean to say, Saturday – I'm flexible. And we were approaching certain disturbing areas back there and, frankly, a crying shame to cut off when we are on the point of some possibly – nitty-gritty. Hmm?

IRISH MAN *nods solemnly.*

Have a little drink and we'll take five.

IRISH MAN. Well, a little one.

JPW. There. Good luck!

IRISH MAN. Cheers!

JPW. Start, stop, cue in, cue out, repeat buttons, nice machine.

IRISH MAN. Was there anything at all in all that talk of yours?

JPW. Frankly, I cannot remember a word of it.

Laughter. JPW closes the door. They are getting quite drunk.
Drinking through the following. Absently, they pull their
chairs to the machine and sit there as if around a fire.

IRISH MAN. You're not married. Just as there's no house,
sylvan dwelling, there's no wife.

JPW. I am enttitled to a little fantasy too.

IRISH MAN. You're not married! – You're not married! –
never were! – Now!

JPW. Isn't your triumph in this discovery excessive?

IRISH MAN. Now! I enjoy our sessions.

JPW. So do I! . . . (*Quietly.*) But there is a woman.

IRISH MAN. Yeh? . . . That brought yeh to your knees? . . .
Not the lady, that nice woman that was here?

JPW (*silently*). No.

IRISH MAN. Yeh?

JPW. You want to talk about me?

IRISH MAN. It's only fair.

JPW. You are not writing a book, Benimillo? Gosh, you are
laughing again!

IRISH MAN. She's a beauty? – Wha'? – Helen – Yeh?

JPW. Yes. Beauty: a shy, simple, comely, virtuous, sheltered,
married maiden.

IRISH MAN. Always the married ones?

JPW. No. I'm unlucky. The discovery that she was already
married deterred me but, after six months of it, I could not
stop myself and I wrote to her my confession of love. Such a
thing to her madonna face was out of the question.

*His laughter, punctuating the story, is pitiful and it sounds
more like crying.*

IRISH MAN. Yeh?

JPW. She requested an interview which I granted in a car park.
The sheltered married maiden's reply to my confession: 'Why
do men always take me by surprise?' I was struck dumb: her
husband apart, I was not the first to notice her beguiling
innocence and domestic potential. When I recovered from the
shock of this, I realised I was serious about her. And I began
a series of written and oral entreaties which were to continue
for a number of years.

IRISH MAN. How many?

JPW. Four. All to no avail . . . The thing was getting out of
hand . . . This simple married maiden was proving to be a
peculiar combination of flirtatious and seductive behaviour
which, having aroused me, instantly turned to resistance and
rejection. She was now my sole goal in life, and I neglected all
else. Would you believe, even a call to Mama's deathbed. I
was otherwise engaged.

IRISH MAN. Two children?

JPW (*nods*). I made a vow: I would celibate myself, keep myself
pure for her. And I added the further precaution of becoming
vegetarian, and eating only health foods. And further, I swore
that if she should come to bed with me for one short hour
and sweet, I would repay her by ending my life there and
then.

IRISH MAN. You told her that?

JPW. Why not? A present of a locket was not going to be of
much use in this case . . . One short sweet hour to allow my
wounds to bleed . . . And I would say to her in the car park,
how remarkable, you and I alive in Time at the same time.
And she would say, but why me? What fate is following me

that wreaks havoc in men's hearts, they lose all care for themselves, their jobs, their everything.

IRISH MAN. She was having a great time.

JPW. She –

IRISH MAN. Oh she was leading you a merry dance.

JPW. No.

IRISH MAN. Oh, I know Irishwomen.

JPW. No.

IRISH MAN. She was making a right fool of you.

JPW. Benimillo! (*Indicating the door.*)

IRISH MAN. And she still is.

JPW. I will not have it! Not from you! You are a very bitter and twisted little man and I'll thank you to keep your opinions to yourself.

IRISH MAN. Okay! Yeh?

JPW. She was very upset.

IRISH MAN. You said it brought you to your knees.

JPW. Did I? Well, it is not finished yet. She phones me every single day!

IRISH MAN. Yeh?

JPW. After a number of final meetings she requested a final meeting. So we met. A hurried meeting: she had even forgotten to take her apron off which I glimpsed beneath her overcoat and which tugged strangely at my heart strings. She said you are a remarkable man and goodbye. Do not regret it, she said, but you must, you *must*, forget me.

IRISH MAN. Regret what?

JPW. You do not understand.

IRISH MAN. Don't regret what, you done nothing.

JPW. Benimillo! We were having an affair with the Gods! And despite the agony I felt a wonder . . . yes, wonder . . . that I should be capable of such sustained intensity about someone and about something for a change . . . Do not regret it, she said, but you must forget me, and though we can never meet again I shall feel energised at every recurrence of your memory. Happiness and beauty are not meant to mate.

IRISH MAN. And that was it?

JPW. Yeh. That evening I met, oh, someone in a supermarket and thus ended four years of celibacy.

IRISH MAN. Aw, they're strange people, women. You can forget her.

JPW. Well, we shall finish *our* little job first, then we shall see. (*He switches on the record-player. Gigli singing 'Toselli's Serenade'.*)

IRISH MAN (*'Wait'll you hear about my one'*). Her name was Ida. (*His gestures, drunkenness, becoming operatic.*)

JPW (*turns down volume a little*). Hmm?

IRISH MAN. Her name was Ida. She had a grand, a lovely speaking voice, d'yeh know, and I felt-a drawn to her without ever having clapped an eye on her.

JPW. She was a radio announcer.

IRISH MAN. Wha'? No! She was a telephonist. I'd never dare go near such a beauty, but, after all, it was on the phone, and I asked her would she like to go for a little walk. The simple way she said yes (*Gave him a great feeling.*). I'd never took a girl out before but I walked happy-as-larry, bliss, Mr King, at her side. Looking at the fountains, the monuments, the – wha'?

JPW *has started muttering, cynically.*

JPW. Milano? Macerata? Recanati?

IRISH MAN. No! Later! Rome! The beggars begging, the English ladies reading poetry, and the lovely little peasant girls that worked as artists' models waiting to be choosed. Wha'?

JPW. Dante? – the poetry – Nothing. You married Ida?

IRISH MAN. No! I had to go 'way. But when I come back I rang the exchange. She didn't work there any more. 'She's been behaving very strange lately,' one of the other telephone girls told me.

JPW. Indiscreet remark from a colleague.

IRISH MAN. Wha'?

JPW. Go on.

IRISH MAN. I ran to her house.

JPW. Dead!

IRISH MAN. No! You-a go way-a ('*You go away.*) her mother said. Please, I said, let me see her. Ida was in hospital.

JPW. Close.

IRISH MAN. She had a nervous breakdown. O-o-o!

JPW. A sore thing.

IRISH MAN. I ran to the hospital and put the little bunch of flowers on her bed and waited for her to laugh or to cry or throw open her arms. But she only turned her head away. Her voice – it didn't sound like a voice at all: tired, faint, d'yeh know, distant. Don't you understand, she said, it's no use.

JPW. Whatever could she mean?

IRISH MAN. I fought them, she said. Them? Her mother and father. I held out for ages, she said, but they said it'd kill them. So I gave in. Then I started fainting all the time, she said, now I'm getting better, but I've promised them.

JPW. 'Promised them what'? (*Mimicking* IRISH MAN.)

IRISH MAN. Never to see you again.

JPW   } 'But why?'!
IRISH MAN } 'But why?' Oh, nothing, she said. You're poor,
             she said, they say I might as well marry a
             beggar, they say you'll end up singing in the
             streets.

JPW. Aha!

IRISH MAN. But, Ida! Don't insist, she said, slow, she said,
  slow. I've changed, she said, it's no use, you see, I don't love
  you no more. I couldn't believe it! I rushed from that room,
  boy. I never saw Ida again.

*His Ida story concludes with the conclusion of 'Toselli's
Serenade' – if possible.*

JPW. What do you think of whore-houses, Benimillo? I could
  recommend a good one. People there dress up as bishops and
  things.

IRISH MAN. But don't yeh see: the similarities between your
  story and mine?

JPW. My story is about a real live living person, your story is
  bullshit. What are you laughing at? (*Beginning to laugh also.*)
  What are you laughing at?

IRISH MAN. One short sweet hour with her, you said, and
  you'd give your life: I'd give my life for one short sweet hour
  to be able to sing like that.

JPW (*privately, not convinced*). Would you?

IRISH MAN (*going out unsteadily*). One short sweet hour.
  (*Off.*) One short sweet hour.

 JPW *alone. He locks the door.*

*Evening light has set in during the above, now further
deepening to night light. Gigli – muted – singing 'Cielo e mar'
timed to conclude with end of the scene.*

JPW. You see, Benimillo, God created the world in order to create himself. Us. We are God. But that neatly done he started making those obscure and enigmatic statements. Indeed his son did a lot of rather the same thing. The Last Supper, for instance: the wine, the conversation, *Jewish* wine being passed around. (*He rises unsteadily.*) Christ standing up, 'In a little while you will see me, in a little while you will not see me.' They must have thought the man was drunk. But he had learned the lingo from his father. God taking his stroll in the Garden, as we were told, and passing by innocent Adam, he would nod, and say (*He nods and winks.*) 'I am who am.' And that was fine until one day, Adam, rather in the manner of Newton, was sitting under a tree and an apple fell on his head jolting him into thought. 'Whatever can he mean,' said Adam, "I am who am"?' And he waited until the next time God came strolling by, and he said, 'Excuse me' – or whatever they said in those days. I must find out. And he put the question to God. But God said, 'Out, out!' 'I only asked!' said Adam. But God said, 'Out!' And, naturally, after such rude, abrupt and despotic eviction, the wind was taken out of Adam's intellectual sails: not surprising that he was not up to pursuing the matter. Which is a pity. Because, the startling thing, God had got it wrong. Because what does it mean, 'I am who am'? It means this is me and that's that. This is me and I am stuck with it. You see? Limiting. What God should have been saying, of course, was 'I am who may be'. Which is a different thing, which makes sense – both for us and for God – which means, I am the possible, or, if you prefer, I am the impossible.

MONA *arrives outside and remains, briefly, to try the door, to knock and call his name. He ignores her and she goes away.*

MONA. Jimmy? . . . Jimmy?

JPW. Yes, it is all crystal clear. We understand our existential guilt, our definition of ourselves is right from the start – I am who may be – and, meanwhile, our paradoxical key, despair,

is rising, rising in our pool to total despair. That state
achieved, two choices. One, okay, I give in, I wait for the next
world. Or, two, what have I to lose, and I take the leap, the
plunge into the abyss of darkness to achieve that state of
primordial being, not in any mudled theocentric sense but as
the point of origin in the *here-and-now* where anything
becomes possible. Now you follow! (*He laughs in
celebration.*) And I have three more days to do it!

*He turns up the volume: 'Cielo e mar', ending this scene
triumphantly.*

Scene Five

*An intermission, if required, has taken place and the quartet
from 'Rigoletto' introduces and continues into this scene.*

*JPW dishevelled and exasperated; IRISH MAN also dishevelled
– unusual for him – bewildered and carrying a hangover. JPW
has locked himself in the washroom: IRISH MAN is banging on
the washroom door.*

IRISH MAN. She's gone, gone, gone, left me!

JPW (*off*). I don't care, I don't care, I don't care!

IRISH MAN. I called last night, you wouldn't let me in! I know
you were in!

JPW (*off*). I was meditating!

IRISH MAN. She took my son!

JPW comes out angrily, clad in a blanket.

JPW. I don't care! Our fourth meeting, two to go and, frankly,
you are confusing and boring the arse off me. (*Striding to the
machine.*) Jesus, that machine! (*Switches it off.*) I went to bed
last night with the repeat button switched on. I woke up and
it was still playing. Heaven knows what it has done to my
brain! And speaking of singing, listen – (*Operating a button*

to the end of the quartet.) Galli Curci: she is quite the best thing on it. (*He listens to the final notes. He switches off the record-player.*) Supernal last note.

IRISH MAN. My wife has left me!

JPW. I don't care! (*He goes to bed.*)

IRISH MAN. She took my son!

JPW. I don't care!

IRISH MAN. Will you listen to me!

JPW. She will have returned home before you this afternoon!

IRISH MAN. I don't want her back!

JPW. So all is well!

IRISH MAN. I'll never forgive her. She says she's afraid I'll hurt the child. I never hurt her! So how can she say such a thing? I thought I was very well when I left here yesterday.

JPW. You were drunk.

IRISH MAN. I thought I was very well last night but it took me by surprise again.

JPW. Ben-i-millo!

IRISH MAN. I started shouting. My son, crying, down the stairs, 'She's only trying to help'. She's only trying to help! It was brave of him, brave little boy, yes, but she's only trying to help. She'd went upstairs, haggard face, up to bed, only trying to help me? And I was feeling very well.

JPW. You were drunk.

IRISH MAN. Wha'? I *roared* at the child. Obscenities. Brave little boy. But now she'd got her suitcase. And took him with her. His face to the back windscreen, driving away, tears running down his face, waving bye-bye, bye-bye, like a baby.

And I just stood there, the lights driving away, don't go, don't go.

JPW. You are a terrible drinker. You're a *terrible* drinker!

IRISH MAN. Wha'? I told you I was! It's not my problem.

JPW (*sharing the last of a bottle with him*). Well, it is a problem this morning.

IRISH MAN. And I left my Gigli record here with you.

JPW. Here, the last hair of the dog.

IRISH MAN (*takes glass unconsciously*). I wouldn't hurt my child.

JPW. Now it is Sunday morning and you arrived – what? – three hours early and, great lapsed churchgoing people that we are, half of this city is still sensibly in its bed. But you have got me up and, double-time or not, I want something more for my endeavours, so . . . Yes! Sex, if you please.

IRISH MAN. I don't *think* I would hurt my son. Or her.

JPW. I'll give you a kick-off then. My first sexual encounter was in mixed-infants.

IRISH MAN. My wife –

JPW. Only matters sexual now or I-shall-not-listen!

A silent contest of wills.

IRISH MAN. . . . Maisie Kennedy.

JPW. Yes?

IRISH MAN. She took me to the end of our garden where the potatoes were.

JPW. Yes?

IRISH MAN. Well, she, then, sort of, took me down on top of her, so that we become hid between the drills, and she kept putting sweets into my mouth while she was trying to get my . . .

JPW. You're doing fine.

IRISH MAN. Trying to get my – my micky into her.

JPW. Yes?

IRISH MAN. I enjoyed the sweets but my micky was too young to repay her treat.

JPW. Very good – you see? – you are quite normal.

IRISH MAN. Sex has nothing to do with it!

JPW. Don't stop now – let it all come out – Your first time, what was that like?

IRISH MAN. I was twenty-two.

JPW. I was twenty-three, clumsy affair – Sorry.

IRISH MAN. I got very excited, and I almost ran, hurrying home to tell Danny. Danny was next in age to me, I was the youngest and I think he was always a bit embarrassed by my – innocence, I think. He was asleep, but I was proud of myself and I wanted to tell him so that he'd see I wasn't a fool. And I woke him up and told him I'd – had it. And he just rolled over and said, 'how many times' and went back to sleep . . . You see, Danny (*'There's a story.'*) . . . You see, my eldest brother had singled out Danny as the one to be put through school, educated. But I don't think school suited our Danny. But I don't think my eldest brother wanted to admit that. But my father sick, and then dying, and my eldest brother had took over, and he become a sort of tyrant.

JPW. That would be Abramo?

IRISH MAN. Mick. Mick frightened us all. Shouting, kicking his bike. Kicking the doors, shouting. My mother thought the world of him. He used to parade his learning too. 'Can

anyone tell me what was St Bernadette's second name?'
'Soubrou', or whatever it was. Imagine, he used to give
Danny tests. In arithmetic, I suppose. And I'd be sitting
quietly, hoping that Danny, locked upstairs in that room,
would pass Mick's examination paper . . . And Danny was
always trying to teach me – cunning, I think. Street sense. He
used to tell me never trust anyone, and that everything is
based on hate. He used to tell me that when I got big, if I was
ever in a fight with Mick, to watch out, that Mick would use
a poker. I suppose he knew he'd never be able for Mick,
unless he shot him, or knifed him. But we didn't do things
that way . . . I wanted to be a priest. I was crazy, I was
thirteen. But some notion in my head about – dedicating? –
my life to others. But Mick, in consultation with my mother –
and rightly so – said wait a couple of years. And one day –
and the couple of years weren't up – and Mick was in a black
mood. And he'd beaten Danny that day too for something or
other, and I had went outside. Oh, just outside, sitting on the
patch of grass. And. There's only two flowers for children
from my kind of background. The daisy and the . . . the
yellow one.

JPW. Primrose.

IRISH MAN. The primrose too – the buttercup. Oh, just sitting
there, picking them off the grass. And Mick come out. What
about the priesthood, he said. I'd changed my mind but I
didn't tell him. I said – I stood up. The couple of years isn't
up I said. But he knew I'd changed my mind and he said
you're stupid, and he flattened me. I knew what he was at, I
was learning. That day the priesthood would've gave the
family a bit of status. But unfortunately for the family, that
day I'd changed my mind . . . Oh yes, the flowers. And. I still
had this little bunch of flowers. In my hand. I don't think I
gave a fuck about the flowers. A few – daisies, and the –
yellow ones. But Danny – he was eighteen! – and he was
inside, crying. And it was the only thing I could think of. (*He
is only just managing to hold back his tears.*) And. And. I
took the fuckin' flowers to our Danny . . . wherever he is now

. . . and I said, which do you think is nicest? The most beautiful, yeh know? And Danny said 'Nicest?', like a knife. 'Nicest? Are you stupid? What use is nicest?' Of what use is beauty, Mr King?

JPW (*gently*). Two million pounds later, Benimillo?

IRISH MAN. Actually, a little more.

JPW. James, Jimmy.

IRISH MAN. But I've strayed from your subject, Mr King.

JPW. That's okay. Would you like a cup of tea?

> IRISH MAN *nods*.

> And I bet you had no breakfast. Tck! You need your food. (*He has got up again and put on his trousers.*)

IRISH MAN. I think I should go home. (*But he does not move.*) Do you have brothers and sisters?

JPW. No. Just me.

IRISH MAN. And you never went back to see your mother before she died?

JPW. Oh, Mama's not dead. She tried to take her life when Father died. She loved him. Though their worlds were worlds apart. But they brought her back. Or she came back. Extraordinary really, because she was always rather delicate. And apparently she was calling my name.

IRISH MAN. Why didn't you go back since?

JPW. Not with tail between my legs, Benimillo. What did your brother do, the authoritative one, Mick?

IRISH MAN. Oh, something the equivalent of shovelling shit.

JPW. Let me clear some of these things out of the way. A frustrated young man –

IRISH MAN. He wasn't a young man, he was in his thir – (*Thirties.*) He wasn't a young man.

JPW. Do you take sugar? Mick was hardly twenty at the time. There was a fattening bag of 'comelackt shoekree erin' (*Comhlucht Siuicre Eireann, sugar*.) about the place at one point.

IRISH MAN. I don't feel inclined to forgive anyone. And I'll never forgive her for last night.

He continues motionless through the following, all the time faced towards the window or the doorway. JPW preparing tea.

JPW. Kettle? (*Which is in his hand.*) That's the kettle. Water? (*Checks the kettle.*) That's water. (*He plugs in the kettle.*) Yes. And Mama, though I was otherwise engaged when she was calling, would know that I loved her. Yes. Now to wash my best china.

He goes to washroom with two mugs.

IRISH MAN. Sum up?

JPW (*off*). What?

IRISH MAN (*beginnings of a roar*). Sum up!

JPW (*off*). Oh! I think you are a basso!

IRISH MAN (*a hiss*). I hate! I f-f-f-f-h-h-h-ate . . .

His hand clutching something in his pocket. A few whimpers escape . . . fixed, rooted in his position, he starts to shout, savage, inarticulate roars of impotent hatred at the doorway . . . developing into sobs which he cannot stop . . . He is on his hands and knees. Terrible dry sobbing, and rhythmic, as if from the bowels of the earth. JPW emerging, slowly, wide-eyed from the washroom. The sobbing continuing.

JPW. Yes . . . yes . . . that's it, Benimillo . . . that is what it is like . . . Let it come out . . . Let it all come out . . . Take my hand . . . if you so wish to . . . We all love you, Benimillo . . . Very good . . . That is very good.

IRISH MAN (*sobs subsiding into tears*). Sorry.

JPW. I know.

IRISH MAN. I'm sorry.

JPW. I know.

IRISH MAN. I'm sorry.

JPW. I know . . . and you are so tired . . . I know.

IRISH MAN. To sing? To sing?

JPW. I know. We'll do it.

IRISH MAN. To sing. (*The sobbing finished, tears and laughter. He is lying on the bed.*)

JPW. Goodness gracious! . . . What! . . . Good heavens! I have never heard such crying! What? Good grief! Dear Me! My word! That was some — what! And the kettle is boiling! (*Tending to kettle, making tea.*) And we shall have a little music in a moment. Actually, my worst sexual experience was not my first one, or second, or third. One of those half-virgins. A simple soul, God bless her. But she thought we were destined for the altar and, consequently, she was covering herself against the possibility of a post-marital attack. Because she had not been completely *virgo intacta* for me, her future husband. The stable-boy had got in there when she was only fourteen she told me. 'I think he half done me,' she said, 'but Daddy caught him.' Caught him where, I wonder? Well, my girl, I said, now you can feel secure at last in the fact that you have just been fully done. And I congratulated her on having received from my good self the official stamp and approval of A-one fulfilling sexual intercourse. Her simple face fell. Was that what that was, she said. The startling thing, I was thirty-one years of age at the time. Left me with a few complexes for a while, I can tell you. Now, a little music. (*He switches on the machine: Gigli singing 'Agnus Dei'.*) And the tea . . . Benimillo? . . . Benimillo?

IRISH MAN *is asleep on the bed. JPW covers him with a blanket. Then he sees* IRISH MAN'*s hat, gets an idea, picks it up, hides it. He sits with his tea, reading a book. Lights fading to evening light. JPW switches on his reading lamp. The 'Agnus Dei' cross-fading into 'Cangia cangia tu voglie' by Fasola.* IRISH MAN *waking up. A certain disgust at discovering himself in these surroundings and in JPW's bed.*

JPW. Awake at last. You needed that sleep . . . Hmm?

IRISH MAN *asks silently for permission to wash his hands in the washroom. He exits to washroom.*

Sum up? Or shall I make some fresh tea? . . . The truth is, we have become fast friends . . . What?

Church clock chiming eight. IRISH MAN *enters. A brief look about for his hat.*

Tomorrow we start transcending a few things, Tuesday you sing . . . Your record! You'll need it tonight.

IRISH MAN *has gone out of door.*

See you tomorrow! . . . Twelve o'clock?

But IRISH MAN *is gone. The four walls, the vodka bottle empty. He considers the phone. Makes usual adjustment to connection-box, then changes his mind about making phonecall (but forgets to make readjustment to the connection-box). He produces* IRISH MAN'*s hat and sits, tie dangling unconsciously from his hand. Gigli sings on, 'Cangia, cangia, tu voglie' to its conclusion.*

Scene Six

Office empty, record-player switched off, church clock chiming twelve. JPW comes hurrying in. He has added the old tie to affect a less casual dress and he is wearing IRISH MAN'*s hat. He is pleased that he has got back to his office on time and is arranging himself in anticipation of* IRISH MAN'*s call. He switches on the record-player. A paper bag from his pockets and a quarter bottle of vodka . . . waiting . . . loosens his tie . . . has a swig of vodka . . . Looking out of the door, the window . . .*

JPW. Benimillo . . . Benimillo . . .

Gigli singing 'Puisqu'on ne peut pas fléchir'. Lights fading.

Scene Seven

The door is open.

IRISH MAN *arriving angrily.* JPW *asleep.*

IRISH MAN. Mr King!

JPW. Hmm?

IRISH MAN. Mr King!

JPW. Who is that?

IRISH MAN. I'd like to have a word with you.

JPW. What time is it?

IRISH MAN. Mr King!

JPW. Come in.

IRISH MAN. I'm in! (*He switches off the machine.*)

JPW (*fully awake*). Benimillo! Come in, my friend, sit down!

IRISH MAN. I'll stand if you don't mind.

JPW. Benimillo!

IRISH MAN. Mr King –

JPW. Have I got stories for you, have I got the goodies for you!

IRISH MAN. Mr King! –

JPW. You never let me get a word in edgeways!

IRISH MAN. Mr King, this has gone on too long. But before I go into that, I'd like to say something about yesterday.

JPW. What day is today?

IRISH MAN. You may think you can read my mind, well, you can't.

JPW. What?

IRISH MAN. Better men have tried and failed. Bigger men and better games than this – or trying to influence me with trickster stuff, hypnosis and the likes, I suppose – well, you can't. I'd lose you and find you. I know what you've been up to.

JPW. Oh, yesterday! I shouldn't feel embarrassed about yesterday.

IRISH MAN. I'm not – Do I look embarrassed to you?

JPW. Emotional incontinence. People break down here all the time, my friend.

IRISH MAN. Who broke down?

JPW. Korky the cat then perhaps?

IRISH MAN. Oh yes, cheap cracks, jokes –

JPW. I thought we had a terrific day yesterday!

IRISH MAN. Listen, I'd just like you to know for one thing, boy, that I had a very happy childhood, you'd like to suggest otherwise, but I'm up to you. Deprived of my father, yes, but my mother, my mother, the Lord have mercy on her, *liked* my father very much, and I often seen her crying. Often, she'd tell me, tears in her eyes, how my father was good to his mother when his mother was old and decrepit, tears in her eyes – how my father slept in the same room – the same bed! – as his mother to nurse and look after her every need. Tears in

my mother's eyes telling me that, boy. A very happy
childhood.

JPW. That's good! You are already on the next stage,
transcending, celebrating the past. (*Offering him a drink.*)

IRISH MAN. Celebrating the — No, I don't want your drink —
and then on to dirty stories and then pumping me for more
information. And Mick — Mick! — Mick was a good singer —
when he wanted to. 'The Snowy-breasted Pearl', boy.
Thought I'd let you know.

JPW. Did your wife return?

IRISH MAN. What! Is that any business of yours? Wasting my
time and my money as if it grew on the trees. I should have
done it myself like I always done, but what a fool, I came to
you. Why are you smiling?

JPW. I'm not. (*But he is inclined to laugh.*)

IRISH MAN. Mr King — Mr King! You done nothing. Now I
think I deserve something more for my time and money.
Before I go, is-there-anything-you-can-tell-me? Why are you
laughing? . . . You're laughing because you don't know or
there's something funny?

JPW. I thought you weren't going to show up!

IRISH MAN. That's all you can say?

JPW. Well, has anyone told you you look twenty years younger
since you started coming to me?

IRISH MAN. They haven't. Anything else?

JPW. Well, you do.

IRISH MAN. And that's it? Pathetic. I told you at the start I
have little or no time for psychiatrists, now I have none
whatsoever for quacks. And, yes, my wife is back. And, yes, I
made my first attempt for months to make conversation with
her at lunchtime. I told her I was simply bored to distraction:

she took it as a reflection on herself and left the room in tears. You're not able to explain that either, I suppose? I left her there – why wouldn't I? – and drove out into the country for myself, the first time in months, beautiful nature all around me, fine sites for development. Will I build a thousand more? No, I've made up my mind on that one. There's more to life than working myself to death or wheeling and dealing with that criminal band of would-be present-day little pigmy Napoleons we've got at the top. Let them have the profit. I need a breath of fresh air. Stopped the car to get out and my only other last hat blew away – (*Sees his hat.*) – Jesus, there's the other one! Well fuck the fuckin' hats! (*He throws the hat from him.*)

JPW. Bis! Bis!

IRISH MAN. What? Hah?

JPW. I did not expect it until tomorrow, but not quite Gigli yet.

IRISH MAN. Look, Mr King, be warned. I could have you locked up, like that, one telephone call. But why go throwing good money after bad. And it was my own fault. I just can't get over what possessed me to come into a place like this when I can cure myself like I did last time.

JPW. Last time?

IRISH MAN. *And* the time before that!

JPW. How often do you get depressed? – Unhappy.

IRISH MAN. Not that it's any of your business, but smart man that you think you are and because I can do what you can't, I'll tell you. Once every year or two. Last time I just went away and hid in a corner – you learn a lot from animals – like a dog in a corner, you couldn't prise me out of it, and stayed there licking my wounds till I cured myself.

JPW. You should have told me.

IRISH MAN. The time before, boy, I went into your territory, debauchery, Mr King: got a dose of the clap in the course of the treatment, but I cured myself.

JPW. And the next time?

IRISH MAN. I'm looking forward to it already!

JPW. You should have told me.

IRISH MAN. About what?

JPW. The pattern!

IRISH MAN. That would have made all the difference, would it?

JPW. You told me you wanted to *sing*!

IRISH MAN. I did! The other times I wanted to do other things.

JPW. Tap-dancing?

IRISH MAN *laughs at him*.

And I told someone this morning that this was a once-off do-or-die aspiration, that there was no pattern – because that is what you told me! – and how astonishing it would be to achieve it.

IRISH MAN. And so much for your confidentiality, hah?

JPW. I'd be wary of the next one, Benimillo.

IRISH MAN. I must remember that. Charlatan, quack, parasite! And, yeh know, there's a stink in this pig-sty: you'd be better off cleaning it up. Sum up?

JPW. . . . Yes. Last year, ladies, debauchery and the clap, this year, grand opera and me. And I *done* nothing? (*Producing books from various places.*) Here, these are yours. Kiekegaard, you read it, make sense of it, stolen out of the South Side Library. Here, Jung, Freud, Otto Rank, Ernest Becker, Stanislav Grof, anonymous donations to your cause,

courtesy of Eason's, Greene's – Trinity College! Heidegger,
try sitting up all night with him for jolly company. What's
this? No! No, you have this one already: *Memoirs of
Beniamino Gigli* – Ida treated him badly all right. Wait! (*He
slams the door shut.*) This is your property, you hired me to
procure it and there is not a decent library or bookshop in
Dublin that I have not shadily visited to get it for you. I'm
summing up, it's my turn, and it is only fair.

Do you know how hard it is to get an appointment with a
psychiatrist at short notice? I managed *two* this morning. I, as
you, arrived early for one appointment and saw the chief
himself going into his office. I slipped in after him, wearing
your hat, my hand in my pocket – like you do it. The chief
thought he was in for it! I dropped to my knees, my hands in
the air, to reassure him. I said I want to sing like Gigli, my
father is a cobbler, bis-bis-bis, can you help me? The chief, in
a whisper, 'Just a mo. Excuse.' Luckily I went to the keyhole,
he was rounding up his men and deputising others to prepare
a padded cell. They nearly nabbed me. Out the front door, in
the back, met by the pursuing posse, out again, three times
round the garden, hid in a bush, the berberis family – look at
the scratches! Until I figured they had figured I had escaped.
But I had to get in there again, an official appointment for a
quarter to ten. Could not risk the front door, or the back, so
what was there to do! In through the window of the waiting
room. Two waiting patients left – *cured*! Sweated it out
behind the *Beano* until I was called to the third-assistant
psychiatrist's office where I – you – *Mickeleen O'Loughlin*
had an appointment.

The psychiatrist was a lady, in years just a little over-ripe,
but that was the last thing on my mind. I want to sing like
Gigli, I was born in Recanati, bis-bis-bis, can you help me?
Was I homosexual? I told her about Ida. Was I *sure* I was not
homosexual? She had at this stage taken off her not-very-
sensible shoes for-a-lady-of-her-years under the desk, and was
now removing her spectacles to suck them slyly sideways.
'Tell me, Mr O'Loughlin, what do you expect of me?' she
said softly. I misinterpreted – I was losing my nerve: I told

her I thought she was beautiful. No, she said, did I expect
medication, analysis or therapy from her. Could I have a glass
of water and an aspirin, please, I said, and while I had her
occupied, I was stealing the six sheets that I now needed from
her prescription pad. Goodness knows what the aspirin was, I
have not been feeling well all day. But I took it – *loudly*! –
demonstrating my great preference above all else for
medication. Because we, Benimillo, had been most remiss,
neglecting so completely to enlist the power of medication to
sing like Gigli, and I set to pumping her on the subject. Oh,
and do you know her fees? Thirty pounds! – Hmmm? – For
twenty-five minutes! I thought it was all for free! Cheque or
cash? Send the bill, I said – Gave my correct address too – I
just could not think fast enough: the surprise that one could
make enormous fortunes at this game, plus the further
complication, the chief's voice once more in the hall: he was
now calming down his men, and they were nearly back to
normal. But I could not risk it: they are most dedicated
people, and I did not have the further strength to run if they
got excited again. So, thank you, to the good lady, and
excuse, as I slipped out to the rose-garden through *her*
window.

IRISH MAN. I'm sorry.

JPW. Not at all.

IRISH MAN. I'm –

JPW. Not at all.

IRISH MAN. I didn't think –

JPW. All part of the service.

IRISH MAN. I'll call you tomorrow.

JPW. No tomorrow.

IRISH MAN. I didn't mean –

JPW. You did mean! I-have-not-finished! Here, these, also, are
for you – (*The small paper bag he returned with: pills.*)
Sweeties, on forged prescriptions. Insidon, anti-downers, one
three times daily will get you to a high C. If you should find
that they do not get you through the day singing – where's
my topper-up? – Here, Nobrium – Excellent name for this
kind of stuff whoever thought it up. And what are these? –
Here – No, these are for myself: Frisium, to put bounce back
into my hair (*He takes some.*) – and to tranquillise my nerves.
Sorry, but I really need these because I have not had a
moment's peace or a decent hour's sleep since I clapped eyes
on you.

IRISH MAN. Jimmy.

JPW. No! You did mean! And you are quite right to walk in
here four hours late. It is a pig-sty, I am a charlatan and a
quack, and I have *never* achieved *anything* in my life! And
stupid, you left out that one. I even learned the baritone role
of the duet on that thing – and I am the tenor! – thought we
might give it a whirl together tomorrow. *I-am-the-tenor!*

IRISH MAN. I spoke out of turn.

JPW. And that gun that you have been terrifying me with.

IRISH MAN. What gun?

JPW. And I am sure there will be a warrant out for my arrest.

IRISH MAN. What gun?

JPW. Your trump card, the final word, that gun in your pocket
that you have been threatening to shoot yourself with, or me
– I never knew which.

IRISH MAN. These? (*He produces a small cylindrical container
of pills.*) Mandrax, sleeping pills. (*He dumps them in the
waste-paper basket.*)

JPW. . . . Do you think you have *got* me then?

IRISH MAN. No.

JPW. Do you think you have won?

IRISH MAN. No. No.

JPW. Well, you have not! Have you seen it through?

IRISH MAN. I'll call –

JPW. Is this what you call seeing it through?

IRISH MAN. I'll call and see you –

JPW. Well, you have not!

IRISH MAN. When you have cooled down.

JPW. You have not!

IRISH MAN. When you have –

JPW. Rather not. No! . . . No.

IRISH MAN *goes out.*

You have not won, Benimillo. I have not finished.

He switches on record-player. Gigli singing 'Tu che a Dio spiegasti l'ali' from 'Lucia De Lammermoor', with bass and chorus. He emits a few pitiful howls in attempt at singing. The telephone rings. He approaches it cautiously, like a man approaching a trap and lifts the receiver.

Hello? . . . Who? . . . Helen? . . . Helen! Are you still there? . . . Fine . . . I have been very fine. (*Silently, 'Helen!'*) . . . No, I'm still here, I just cannot, I mean to say – Helen! . . . What? . . . Music. Beniamino Gigli . . . You've heard of him? Really? (*Celebratory laugh.*) Born in Bunratty! (or, Killarney) . . . No, I'm laughing because, I mean to say, how are you? . . . What is the matter? . . . Why are you crying? . . . Why are you . . . Pardon? . . . I did not phone you yesterday because . . . I did not phone you the day before because . . . You asked me not to. To promise, not to call you. What? . . . (*Shocked.*) I am a *what*? . . . Dirty? I never made a dirty phonecall to you . . . And if I ever call you again you shall

. . . Send the police! . . . Hello? . . . Hello? (*He puts down the phone.*) Bloody hell.

He is stunned . . . He remembers the Mandrax and is on his hands and knees searching the waste-paper basket for them. MONA arrives.

MONA. Well, lover! Some batteries for your shaver and a present.

She puts batteries, a pot plant and a bottle of vodka on the desk and she leaves an overnight bag somewhere. She goes to the record-player.

What's this?

JPW (*absently*). I am very busy right now, Mona. Bloody hell. (*He finds the container of Mandrax; he is half-frightened of them; then becoming conscious of MONA, and relieved by her presence. He puts the Mandrax in his pocket.*) Mona! You would not believe it, people are crazy! You are the absolutely only normal human being in the world!

He has come up behind her and circled her waist with his arms. She likes the feeling of his arms around her but the cloud of her secret sadness is moving across her face.

And how is Karen-Marie, your god-child?

MONA. What god-child?

JPW (*not listening*). Isn't that interesting?

The music is cross-fading from 'Tu che a Dio spiegasti l'ali' to 'Caro mio ben', leading into the final scene.

Scene Eight

JPW *and* MONA *dressed as before –* MONA *minus her overcoat and gloves – lying on the bed, something childlike about them, huddled together, eyes on the record-player, listening to the music. Gigli singing 'Caro mio ben' followed by 'Amarilli'.*

MONA. That's the fourth – fifth? – time round. You could go away for a year with that thing switched on and it would still be playing when you got back.

JPW. Yeh.

MONA. What's he singing, what's he saying now?

JPW. You don't have to know, whatever you like.

MONA. Beloved.

JPW. If you like.

MONA. That everything ends.

JPW. Yes. But that at least we end up friends. At least that.

MONA. That everything ends anyway. And does it matter – does-it-matter! – if it all ends now, a few seconds earlier, for God's sake! . . . Jimmy.

He offers her the bottle of vodka absently. She declines. She looks at her watch.

JPW. That you are breathing, now, this moment . . . alive in Time at the same time as I . . . and that I can only hold my breath at the thought.

MONA. That's nice.

JPW. Beloved.

MONA. Why don't you call me that? . . . There's someone or something wounding you very deeply, and I can't do a thing about it.

JPW (*a new thought*). No. That is what I *used* to think. (*Offering her the bottle again.*) *You* and I are alive in Time at the same time.

MONA. I'm not meant to. (*Then she changes her mind, a silent 'fuck it' and she takes a swig.*) Why do you put up with it?

JPW. You're not listening to me.

MONA. When life is —

JPW (*celebratory laugh*). Bouncing back! Isn't that interesting? Bother the lot of them!

MONA. When life is short. And *I'm* here. Well — (*About to qualify the last, changes her mind.*) Some bird you want to screw, is it? I'd do that for you in a wheelchair on the fucking moon. The way some of you mope about. I know you think I'm vulgar.

JPW } No. I think you are —
MONA } Well, I am not — Oh, fuck it, maybe I am! But all our family is! Brothers, sisters, Mammy, Daddy — ten of us! — You should hear us all together! — We're all vulgar!

JPW. What are you talking about?

MONA. I'm talking about — All that energy about! Why are people moping? All that energy in the world, to be enjoyed, to kill pain, to give to the children.

JPW. What's wrong?

MONA (*She has another long swig of vodka*). And watch them grow up.

JPW. You are not listening.

MONA. . . . . I'm listening to you. (*Her eyes on the machine.*) Do you know what he's (*Gigli.*) saying? A baby. That's what it's all about.

JPW. The farmer's wife! (*He is looking at her, seeing her potential.*) And a lot of easy money to be made in farming. I could be a farmer.

MONA *laughs.*

Well, it's possible.

MONA. That's what you said to me in the supermarket, anything is possible.

JPW. We are a very good team, Mona.

MONA. Too late.

JPW. Hmmm?

MONA. You wouldn't be able to buy a farm now anyway. Why didn't you invest your money?

JPW. Yes, well, but. I'm glad you're here.

MONA. I know. I feel it for the first time.

JPW. Do you? (*'Isn't that interesting?'*) What are you looking at your watch for?

MONA. I wasn't. I got a letter from my young sister today, do you want to hear?

JPW. Yes. Bother the lot of them. (*He switches off the machine.*) And if he comes back for that (*Machine.*) I'll have it hocked, tell him it was stolen. (*He lies beside her again.*)

MONA. Here's a bit. This is the hospital where she works and there's this young doctor, and he was passing remarks about 'the pips' under Caroline's uniform. All of us are like that too, up here. (*Small-breasted.*) The girls, that is, (*Reading.*) '. . . the pips under my uniform and I said you wouldn't like one of them up your arse as a pile, would you. So the laugh was on him.' I told you! We all talk like that. (*Suddenly grave.*) But you should see our Caroline. She's beautiful.

JPW. Like you.

MONA. 'Daddy made custard two nights ago and, mind you, it was very nice. So he made it again last night. It was like soup, all lumpy, and no one could eat it. So we gave it to the dogs. All the dogs had their feet in the air in the morning.' It's nice to get a letter when you're not expecting it. Jimmy, I have cancer. I've been going to doctors for another purpose, but life is full of surprises.

JPW. Breast cancer? (*Motionless – and continues so through the following.*)

MONA. Tck, no! You should know that. The pancreas. I wanted to lie beside you for a while. I've been delaying. I've to go in a minute. I go in tonight to start the treatment. My husband – honestly, that man! – started crying, would you believe, when I told him. Silly c – sorry – clunt. Oh for God's sake, I said, I'm-Not-Dead-Yet! (*Aside to him.*) Hard to kill a bad thing. Will you send me flowers?

JPW *nods.*

(*Getting up.*) And, if the worst comes to the worst, as they say – (*A movement to restrain her from getting up.*) I have to go, Jimmy – I have no regrets. (*Dressing, overcoat, gloves through the following.*) Well, a few. I had a little girl when I was sixteen. They didn't mean to, but now I know they pressurised me. They wanted the father's name. I wouldn't give it. They needed it to have her adopted. I wouldn't give it. Still, they had her adopted some way. Things hadn't gone right, complications, and I was very ill. I only saw her twice. She was so tiny. She's twenty-two now. Somewhere. I've been trying to repeat the deed ever since. I picked you up. And if I had had a child by you, or any of the others, I don't think I would have told you. I'd have been the one you wouldn't have seen for dust. Pregnant into the sunset. But preferably by you. Others weren't so gentle in how they – regarded me. But it couldn't be done. And maybe just as well now. So I invented a modest god-child, in some kind of – fancy? – in the meantime, to keep me going. But Karen-Marie. Yeh. Maybe just as well now. Well, my magician friend, am I forgetting anything? (*An imperative:*) Water that! (*The potted plant.*) See yeh.

He nods.

Beloved?

He nods.

I love you.

She leaves. He switches on the record-player, blasting up the volume – Elizabeth Rethberg/Gigli/Pinza singing the trio 'Tu sol quest anima' from 'Attila'. He is now crying, shouting at the door.

JPW. I love! I love you! Fuck you! I love! Fuck you! I love! – I love! Fuck you – fuck you! I love . . .

Gigli's voice now taking over from Rethberg's and JPW appears to be finding a purpose out of the blaring singing. He remembers the container of Mandrax in his pocket and he takes a couple, does not like the taste and washes them down with a swig of vodka. A sudden stomach cramp but he recovers quickly.

Silhouette of IRISH MAN *arriving.* JPW *does not hear him come in.* IRISH MAN *entering – his entrance timed with bass solo in the trio from 'Attila'. He is dressed in tuxedo, smoking a cigar, has had a few drinks. He is unsure about* JPW's *attitude, whether or not it is to be taken as banter. He has a present of a bottle of vodka. His first lines are spoken under the music.* JPW, *in half doubled-up position, continues motionless for some time.*

IRISH MAN. Can I come in? I drank you out of house and home the other day. I was a bit shy, hesitating about calling. Can we have a little one together? Will I open this, or – (*He takes the bottle already opened.*) Waste not, want not, and you'll have a little store in for yourself. (*He puts a drink in* JPW's *hand, then switches off the music.*) Aa, the aul' music! The itinerants moved on. Oh, d'yeh mind? (*The cigar.*) They moved on, the creatures. It cost me a few bob but – ah, my place wasn't a suitable place at all for them. Please God they'll find a more suitable site. They have a tough life of it and it's not their fault. (*He sits.*) Oh, d'yeh mind? Just for a minute. But I was doing my sums going home in the car and it come into my head. Supposing my life depended on it, who would I turn to? I went through mothers, brothers, relations. The wife. It all boils down to the wife for us all in the end. So we're going out for the evening. I left her (*Down the road.*)

with some friends for a few minutes. Good luck, God bless, cheers! And I couldn't help thinking – Hah-haa, you're a queer one! – strange as the route you took me, you had some kind of hand in leading me to that conclusion.

JPW. It is Tuesday?

IRISH MAN. No. What?

JPW. Final session.

IRISH MAN (*laughs*). Aw!

JPW. A refund?

IRISH MAN (*laughs*). No!

JPW. But the job is not finished.

IRISH MAN. I'm fine – thanks in some measure to you.

JPW. But it can be done. To sing. The sound to clothe our emotion and aspiration. And what an achievement.

IRISH MAN. The next time, the one you warned me about.

JPW. No, we have tried laughing, and crying, and philosophy.

IRISH MAN. You're a case!

JPW. I have boiled it down to two options. Have you considered surgery?

IRISH MAN. An operation is it?

JPW (*laughing – but quite likely precipitated by a stomach cramp*). You were taking me seriously there. (*Offering to top up his drink.*)

IRISH MAN. No – no – no! I don't know how to take you, Mr King.

JPW. And naughty Benimillo, you have a few in you already.

IRISH MAN. And by the looks of you, you've had more than your share. I'd a drop of champagne. Champagne is light d'yeh know. Was I your first client?

JPW (*absently; looking out of window or door*). No. There was one other. It's pretty bad out there, isn't it?

IRISH MAN. Oh, now.

JPW. Ever returning, waking up, lying down, more unhappy.

IRISH MAN. You can surprise yourself and find yourself strayed too far from the world all right . . . You're looking very pale.

JPW. So I bring my last option into play. Have you considered magic?

IRISH MAN. Mr King –

JPW. You are going to ask me what is magic –

IRISH MAN. Mr King, Mr King!

JPW. Jimmy! Jimmy!

IRISH MAN. Jimmy. Jimmy. And we are friends, and I'm sorry I upset you today, and I'm sorry I have to rush now, but I called because I was wondering if there was some way I could repay all the trouble you took. If there was some way at all?

JPW. It is rest for me to take trouble for a friend.

IRISH MAN. That's it, that's –

JPW. Persian proverb.

IRISH MAN. That's the kind you are but, reality, face the facts. And I'm not talking a hundred or two hundred. A couple of grand, to set you up. You did a great job.

JPW. No, not yet.

IRISH MAN. I could stretch it to three.

JPW. I shan't hold you. I know you have to rush – And don't tell me: you are going on a holiday? I knew it. These little ceremonies can be pleasantly tranquillising. You have taken yourself captive again, but dread still lies nesting, Benimillo.

IRISH MAN (*preparing to go*). Well, I'm very grateful to you.

JPW. No, I am grateful to you. I longed to take myself captive too and root myself, but you came in that door with the audacity of despair, wild with the idea of wanting to soar, and I was the most pitiful of spiritless things.

IRISH MAN. Well.

JPW. Leave it to me, Benimillo.

IRISH MAN. And I did get the right man for the job.

JPW. Oh, and your machine!

IRISH MAN. No, you keep that.

JPW (*logically*) But I shan't require it.

IRISH MAN. Since you'll take nothing else. No, a little gift . . . Go home, Jimmy. Forget that – Irish colleen. You *are* a remarkable man. I know there's kindness in the world, but they'll kill you over here. (*Silently.*) Go home.

He leaves. JPW into action. He locks the door, switches off the record-player, unplugs it from its power-point as a double precaution (and proof). He looks out of the window for a moment, then draws the blind. He goes to his desk where he spreads jam on a slice of bread, cuts the bread into squares and decorates each square with a Mandrax pill. Through the following, a red glow, as if emanating from the reading lamp with the red shade, suffuses the room, and the shaft of yellow light from the washroom becoming more intense.

JPW. You are going to ask me what is magic. In a nutshell, the rearrangement and redirection of the orbits and trajectories of dynamatological whirlings, i.e., simply new mind over old matter. This night I'll conjure. If man can bend a spoon with beady steadfast eye, I'll sing like Gigli or I'll die. Checklist. Too many facts in the world. Addiction to those lies arrested. Rationalisations recognised – yes, you have dallied too long with your destiny. All alibis exhausted, desire for ahievement, mind set on goal. Trump card – (*He pops a square of bread*

*and jam with pill on top into his mouth and washes it down
with vodka.*) And wait. (*After a moment, he opens his mouth
as if to sing. An abortive sound/silence. Another piece of
bread and jam with pill on top . .*) And wait, wait, wait . . .
until the silence is pregnant with the tone urgent to be born
. . . The soul! Of course! The soul of the singer is the
subconscious self. Realistic thinking, honest desire for
assistance. (*To heaven.*) Rather not. You cut your losses on
this little utopia of greed and carnage some time ago, my not
so very clever friend. (*To the floor.*) You, down there! Assist
please. In exchange – (*Another square of bread and jam with
pill into his mouth and washes it down with vodka. Faintly –
and as an echo, from a distance – orchestral introduction for
the aria 'Tu che a Dio spiegasti l'ali'. Whispers:*) What?
Yesss! Thank you. But just a mo. (*Gestures, cueing out music,
takes another pill, and decides against further vodka.*) Stops
taking alcohol, purity of potion, contentment in abstinence,
care of personal appearance, diminishing fears of unknown
future, resolution fixed in mind for possibilising it, increase in
control to achieve it. (*Orchestral introduction begins again.*)
Abyss sighted! All my worldly goods I leave to nuns. Leeep!
(*Leap.*) pluh-unnge! (*Plunge. And a sigh of relief.*) Aah!
Rebirth of ideals, return of self-esteem, future known.

*On cue, he sings the aria to its conclusion and collapses.
(Gigli's voice; the recording he made solo, without bass and
chorus.) JPW on the floor. The church clock chiming six a.m.*

JPW. Mama? Mama? Do not leave me in this dark.

*Some resilience within pulling himself up. Lights returning to
normal. He lets up the blind. Early morning light filtering
into the room. He looks ghastly. He wonders if he is not
dead: a single gasp or grunt to check on this. He remembers
record-player: checks to find that it is indeed disconnected
from its power-point: smile, laugh of achievement. He puts a
few things in an old leather bag and whatever vodka remains
into his pocket. He is about to leave, gets an idea. He opens
the window, plugs in the record-player, switches it on, presses*

repeat button, 'invites' the music towards the open window.
Gigli's 'O Paradiso'.

JPW. Do not mind the pig-sty, Benimillo . . . mankind still has a
delicate ear . . . That's it . . . that's it . . . sing on forever . . .
that's it.

He unlocks the door and goes out, a little unsteady on his
feet.